CONDUCTORS OF THE PIT

CONDUCTORS OF THE PIT
poetry written in extremis in translation

Translated and Edited
by Clayton Eshleman

Soft Skull Press
Brooklyn, NY | 2005

Conductors of the Pit
© 2005 ed. Clayton Eshleman
Cover art by Peter Blegvad
Published by Soft Skull Press | www.softskull.com
Distributed by Publishers Group West | www.pgw.com | 800.788.3123

Book Design: Elizabeth Knafo

Library of Congress Cataloging-in-Publication Data

Conductors of the pit : poetry written in extremis / translated & edited by
Clayton Eshleman.
  p. cm.
 Includes bibliographical references.
 ISBN 1-932360-74-3 (alk. paper)
 1. Poetry, Modern—Translations into English. I. Eshleman, Clayton.

PN6101.C644 2005
808.81'03—dc22

2005003353

Other books by Clayton Eshleman

POETRY
Mexico & North (1962)
Indiana (1969)
Altars (1971)
Coils (1973)
The Gull Wall (1975)
What She Means (1978)
Hades In Manganese (1981)
Fracture (1983)
The Name Encanyoned River (1986)
Hotel Cro-Magnon (1989)
Under World Arrest (1994)
From Scratch (1998)
Everwhat (2003)
My Devotion (2004)

PROSE
Antiphonal Swing (1989)
Companion Spider (2002)
Juniper Fuse, Upper Paleolithic Imagination &
  the Construction of the Underworld (2003)

TRANSLATIONS
Pablo Neruda, Residence on Earth (1962)
César Vallejo, The Complete Posthumous Poetry (with José Rubia Barcia, 1978)
Aimé Césaire, The Collected Poetry (with Annette Smith, 1983)
Michel Deguy, Given Giving (1984)
Bernard Bador, Sea Urchin Harakiri (1986)
Aimé Césaire, Lyric & Narrative Poetry 1946-1982 (with Annette Smith, 1990)
Antonin Artaud, Watchfiends & Rack Screams (with Bernard Bador, 1995)
César Vallejo, Trilce (1992, 2000)
Aimé Césaire, Notebook of a Return to the Native Land
  (with Annette Smith, 2001)

EDITOR
Folio (Bloomington, Indiana, 3 issues, 1959-1960)
Quena (Lima, Peru, 1 issue edited, suppressed by the
  North American Peruvian Institute, 1966)
Caterpillar (NYC-Los Angeles, 20 issues, 1967-1973)
A Caterpillar Anthology (issues #1-12, 1971)
Sulfur (Pasadena-Los Angeles-Ypsilanti, 46 issues, 1981-2000)

Acknowledgements

This translation of Rimbaud's "Drunken Boat" is reprinted from *Conductors of the Pit* (Paragon House, 1988); it originally appeared, in a slightly different version, in *The Gull Wall* (Black Sparrow Press, 1975). The Neruda translations originally appeared, in significantly different versions, in *Residence on Earth* (Amber House Press, 1962); "Sexual Water" and "Only Death" appeared in *Poems for the Millennium*, Volume 1 (University of California Press, 1995). The José Hierro poems appeared in *Quark 1 / Translations from the Spanish* by Clayton Eshleman & Cid Corman (Camels Coming, 1967). Césaire's "Lynch I" was published as part of "At the Locks of the Void: Co-Translating Aimé Césaire" in *Companion Spider* (Wesleyan University Press, 2002). His "Laughable" and the section from "Configurations" were published in *Sulfur* #39 and #45/46. Vallejo's "The Need to Die" appeared in *The Denver Quarterly*, Summer 1994. His "The three hundred womanly states of the Eiffel Tower" appeared in *Sulfur* #45/46. The Radnóti, Juhász, Csoóri, and Szöcs poems appeared, along with the Bollobás Note on Szöcs, in *Sulfur* #21. All of the Bernard Bador poems were published in *Sea Urchin Harakiri* (Panjandrum Press, 1986). The Note on Vladimir Holan and "A Night with Hamlet" were published in *Conductors of the Pit* (1988 version). Artaud's "Revolt Against Poetry" appeared in *Sulfur* #45/46. His "Pounding and Gism" and "Civil Status" were published in *Sulfur* #8. His "Letter to André Breton" (in a slightly different version) appeared as *Sparrow* #23 (1974). "Ten years that the language has been gone" was published as part of "Artaud's True Family, Glimpsed at Pompidou," in *Companion Spider*. "I spit on the innate Christ" and "To be Christ is not to be Jesus Christ" appeared in *American Poetry Review*.

Contents

Introduction

In the Introduction to the smaller 1988 version of *Conductors of the Pit*, with César Vallejo, Aimé Césaire, Antonin Artaud, and Vladimir Holan in mind, I wrote:

> In the course of the 20th century, at certain points on the globe, there has ignited a poetry that goes for the whole, a poetry written in *extremis*, a poetry that attempts to become responsible for all the poet knows about himself and his world. Such poetries challenge all living writers and would-be-writers to break out of easily-adapted molds (the poem as a single lyric object) and to face, as Charles Olson once put it, "the ongoing front of reality."

The title –*Conductors of the Pit*– first occurred as a phrase in my poem written in 1984, "Deeds Done and Suffered by Light, " in the concluding stanza:

> Persephone's a doll
>   steeper than Marilyn,
> miracles lick her,
>   dreams invade her,
> over the cobweb orchestra
>   there's an ice
>   conductor,
> forget the orchestra,
>   conduct the pit!
> Hanged
> Ariadne
>   giving birth in Hades
> is the rich, black music in mother's tit!

The pit, the abyss, the unknown Baudelaire proposed poets are to penetrate, the penetralia, the recesses of the mind, the darkness of political domination, the gulf between worlds. To conduct the pit, then, versus the orchestra of the living, is to induct and order materials from the subconscious as well as from those untoward regions of human experience that defy rational explanation. Parallel universes. Conversations with the dead.

Or simply the price of experience magnificently evoked in this passage from Vladimir Holan's "A Night with Hamlet:"

> I'm still looking for that soup kitchen
> whose food window is not the wicket in a cell door,
> a wicket through which the imprisoned are observed,
> that peephole called the Judas...
> *'Who doesn't work doesn't eat!'* Yes,
> *but what is work? To be true to one's unselfish lot—*
> or to be a salesman of indulgences
> or an ardent stoker of a crematorium,
> to insert a thermometer into the rectum of war
> or to have to sing at a vintage
> as proof that you are not eating the grapes,
> to inspect horses' teeth or like a hangman
> rip out the nostrils of creatures before they swing,
> to be corroded by vinegar and bile and take revenge
>   on others
> or burn off women's right breasts
> to make them better archers,
> to be the seed of fate in the womb of history
> or a feeling sentenced to drudgery
> under the gray Siberia of elderly heads—
> or even under the threat of losing your throat, to file
>   through your chains,
> and rather gouge your eyes out
> that they not see today's horrors,
> and yet to hear those long dead
> but free singers?...

The compositional net at best catches an ornament...

In the 17th century, the rugged mountains of the Alps were still a source of awe and terror to those who beheld them. However, a hundred years later, perhaps as a result of Enlightenment thinking, Jean Jacques Rousseau writes in his autobiography that "he loved to walk in his favorite place in the Savoyan Alps, a path at the edge of a ravine where, secured by a railing, he could look down into the gorge in order to induct a feeling of dizziness

for himself at ease, adding 'I love this whirling, provided that I am in safety.'"
Wolfgang Giegerich comments:

> What changed was the ontological framework within which the same
> sight is seen and from which it receives its nature, its ontological
> quality and status. In the one case, in the earlier century, the ravine was,
> to be sure, just as limited as at the time of Rousseau. But, obviously, it
> was not confined to being merely this one particular thing. Rather, it
> opened up and allowed you to see the abyss of being as such, the pri-
> mordial void, the yawning chaos prior to all creation, cosmological
> Chaos. The one individual gorge was like a window through which all-
> encompassing wilderness was glaring at you and into your life, threat-
> ening to intrude into the insular world of day, hope, and safety. You
> looked at this particular thing, the one ravine there, but what you saw
> in it was all around you, also behind your back, and even in your own
> heart. And thus you were in it; your safety was only the borrowed security
> of a small boat in the ocean of being. It would have been impossible
> during that age to have put a fence around the ravine, because despite
> its limited quantitative size, it was immense, endless, bottomless.[1]

The poetry in this collection, in Giegerich's image, sets a window into the
gorge with a railing, and lets some of its abyssal power glare into the language.
And receiving the abyss is only part of the charge that these poets have
taken on: they have conducted chaos in such a way that it has been sym-
phonically bound into their writing. In this sense, they are not conductors of
the orchestra, but conductors of the pit, snake-charming its depths, draw-
ing up figurations that sway in rhythm to, or against, their own processes.

All of the writers in this collection qualify, in one way or another, as "con-
ductors." To my knowledge, their writing has never before been assembled
side by side. While they all belong to their own schools, or selves alone,
they all strike similar chords via their relationship to "the pit." This doesn't
mean that they are not also, in varying ways, funny, sweet, and very human.
All are uncontaminated by what might be called "official verse culture." All
practice a language that lies out on the dragon's tongue.

While Aimé Césaire is the only one of the poets who has identified himself
as a Surrealist, all, including Césaire, have assimilated Surrealism and
arguably have written as fulgurating and enduring poems as any of the

Surrealist founders. All have what I think of as a healthy ambivalence about all 20th century "movements," and some of the difficulty in reading them is due to their constant refusal to let their psychic wounds heal over. These poetries all have a critical as well as inspirational relationship to Romanticism, and seem in gesture allied to Abstract Expressionism (with the occasional exceptions of Vallejo and Radnóti, all are much more concerned with process rather than product). It occurs to me that their poetries might be thought of as Abstract Romanticism. The problem with any identification is that given the mass of incorporated directions, including Realism, and what Mikhail Bahktin referred to as "Grotesque Realism," no single term seems accurate and inclusive.

All have, from differing perspectives, given differing existential situations, grasped in the works presented here a significant portion of the abyss and met it with assimilative imagination. While all may be shocking, obscure, or lost at moments, such "negations" do not arise out of irony or coyness or a simplistic contempt for the human condition, but are there as an unavoidable consequence of attempting to say their condition as it is invaded by, or abandoned by, the world at large. While they are certainly of our time—poverty-stricken Vallejo confronting his dying in 1937 Paris, Radnóti scribbling love poems to his wife at night in a pocket notebook while dying in a Nazi labor battalion, Césaire summoning courage to take on the Martinican condition, Artaud emerging after nine years of asylum incarceration, Holan erased by the Czech State and hermetically sealed in a house on a tiny island in the center of Prague—they also seem to be somewhat out of our time, as if their voices are strengthened by a connection to the past when men were bound by necessity in a weighted, hopeless present, constantly face to face with a fate that was not the annihilation of fate itself, but a fate that nailed one to something. Wallace Stevens evokes its size in the phrase, "the stale grandeur of annihilation."

My translations or co-translations attempt to reconcile two often incompatible aspects of the art of translation: the need to respect all aspects of the original text, to work within the boundaries that it establishes—while working out improvisational strategies to register such accuracy in language that is fresh, potent, and as captivating as poetry can be written in American English.

The genesis for this book took place after a revision of some of the poetry in *Conductors of the Pit: Major Works by Rimbaud, Vallejo, Césaire, Artaud, and Holan*, published by Paragon House in 1988, and out of print since 1992 when Paragon House went out of business. In the early 1990s, I revised, with the help of Bernard Bador, the Artaud versions from *Conductors* and these, along with additional translations, appeared in *Watchfiends & Rack Screams* (Exact Change, 1995). With co-translator Annette Smith, I reformatted and revised our translation of Césaire's *Notebook of a Return to the Native Land* and it appeared as a single volume published by Wesleyan University Press in 2001. All of the poems in the Vallejo section of *Conductors* can be found (in slightly different versions) in *César Vallejo: The Complete Posthumous Poetry* (co-translated with José Rubia Barcia), University of California Press, 1978.

This left Rimbaud's "The Drunken Boat" and Holan's "A Night with Hamlet" out of print. They became the nucleus for an expanded *Conductors*, which not only contains works by Vallejo, Artaud, and Césaire not in the large, single author collections, but poetry by Pablo Neruda, José Hierro, André Breton, Bernard Bador, Miklós Radnóti, Ferenc Juhász, Sandor Csoóri, and Géza Szöcs. In short, this is a book that fills in more details of my map of translation while linking up with some of the other collections.

As a kind of epigram to the other sections, I offer a new translation of Arthur Rimbaud's "The Drunken Boat," which still seems to me to be a signal gesture toward a trust in the coherence of the subconscious. The "Boat" is at one extreme a poem about running away from home and returning after a few nights in the woods with one's tail between one's legs, sadly eager for a hot meal and a warm bed; at another extreme, as Richard Sieburth has pointed out in a letter to me, the whole poem swings between Genesis and Apocalypse. It is also an early and stunning use of collage that anticipates what Robert Duncan has identified, for our times, as the "grand collage," and it is the first modern recognition in which I am aware of the extent to which the poem that goes for everything is bound to fail. Implicit in this recognition is the size of loss involved in all genuine explorations. *Think of it in this context as a flag carried swiftly through a clearing in the forest before the horsemen break into view.*

Mainly through Jack and Ruth Hirschman, I discovered foreign language poetries at the same time that I discovered American poetry in the late

1950s at Indiana University. Pablo Neruda's first two *Residencia en la tierra* collections were the first poems, in translation, to get under my skin. In my first poetry reading, participating in the Hirschman-directed "Babel" series, I read translations from St.-John Perse's *Eloges*. Hitchhiking to Mexico the summer of 1959, inspired by Neruda, subsequently led to long residences in Japan, Peru, and France.

A small edition of my Neruda translations was published in 1962 by the short-lived Amber House Press in San Francisco. The book has never been reprinted. When I decided to assemble the new *Conductors of the Pit*, I was faced with a decision: to either reprint some of these versions, or to retranslate them. Since I go into this matter at length in the Appendix to this book, I will not discuss Neruda here, other than to say ideally I would have liked to print the old versions side by side with the revisions. Every translator has to begin somewhere, and it is possible that a comparative reading of 1962 *Residencia* translations with 2002 versions might help a young translator to find his or her way.

The two José Hierro poems were done with Cid Corman in Kyoto in 1963. After my Neruda adventure, I decided that I could learn something about translating working together with Cid. His translations of Montale, Celan, Char and Bashō (appearing at this time in *origin* magazine, second series) felt accurate and read very well. I no longer recall why we decided to work together on the Spanish Hierro nor do I have the book any longer that we translated from. Working together with Cid, I realized that I had been taking short-cuts with my Neruda translating, guessing at words when I was not sure of their meaning, leaving things out when they appeared to be flat in English, and thinking too much of a translation as a kind of Eshleman poem. Corman taught rigorous respect for the original text, including line breaks (when possible), and the necessity of researching difficult and rare words. He brought across to me an image of the translator as a translator-scholar, one whose role was to guard, in the act of translating, the integrity of the original and to trust that it knew what it was doing (and thus did not need to be "corrected" by the translator). Corman prepared me for the challenges I would face in Vallejo's *Poemas humanos* (and he went over many of my versions of those poems with me in their early drafts).

The four Vallejo prose poems are to be found in the 1991 *Obras completas, Tomo 1, Obra poética*, Banco de Crédito del Peru, edited by Ricardo Gonzáles Vigil, and the 1988 *Poesía completa, Casa de las Americas, Ciudad de la Habana*, edited by Raúl Hernández Novás. "The Need to Die" first appeared in El Norte, Trujillo, March 22, 1926. The other three pieces were published for the first time in *Contra el secreto profesional*, edited by the poet's widow in 1973; they belong with the dozen or so prose poems Vallejo appears to have written in Paris in the mid-1920s (the rest are translated in *The Complete Posthumous Poetry*). I co-translated the first two pieces with the Peruvian novelist, Jorge Guzmán.

I discovered Aimé Césaire in the second issue of Jack Hirschman's tiny *Hip Pocket Poems*, 1960. Césaire's prose poem, "Lynch I," since edited out of the 1948 *Soleil cou coupé* (*Solar Throat Slashed*), was translated by Emile Snyder, a French transplant who was an early translator of Césaire. The poem sank into me like a depth charge. Emile's translation was adequate, but a close scrutiny of it and the original revealed that he had simplified a few of the poem's erudite words and tropes, so I retranslated it in 1995 during the O.J. Simpson trial.

In its "logic of metaphor" chain reaction, its linking of social terror with the violence of sudden natural growth, and its sacrifice of a male hero for the sake of sowing the seeds of renewal, "Lynch I" is a typical and very strong Césaire poem of the late 1940s. For years I didn't know what to make of it, yet its strangeness was mesmerizing. It seemed to imply that for the speaker to suddenly deeply inhale, to offer himself to the wild, was to induct the snapping of a lynched neck. Erotic aspects of the poem came to mind in the 1970s when I saw the Japanese film *Realm of the Senses*, in which the sex-addicted male lead makes his partner choke him to wring the last quiver out of his orgasm.

The other two Césaire translations (co-translated with Annette Smith) are from an unpublished (as a book) series of twenty-two poems, "Comme un malentendu de salut," collected at the end of Césaire's definitive 1995 *La Poésie*. Written in the 1980s and early 90s, these appear to be the last poems that the poet, born in 1913, has published. Like the poems in the 1982 Moi, laminaire (I, *laminaria*, part of our 1990 *Lyric and Dramatic Poetry: 1946-1982*, from the University Press of Virginia), "Laughable" and "from *Configurations*" are austere "late-style" writing that contrasts remarkably with Césaire's lush and dense surrealistically-geared poetry of the 1940s and 1950s.[2]

The ten poems of Bernard Bador are from a selected poems that I translated of his, with his help, in the early 1980s: *Sea Urchin Harakiri* (Panjandrum Books, 1986, with a Postface by Robert Kelly). After Jess, Bador is the most imaginative paste-up collagist whose work I am familiar with. Born in Lyon, and educated to be a lawyer, Bador lived in Los Angeles for many years, managing a rubber tire patch factory. Several years ago he returned to the Beaujolais region where he has converted an old wine vat barn into a studio, library, and living quarters. While Bador's poetry is genuinely bizarre, I also find it hilarious at times, and I have never laughed so much with another person as when I was translating *Sea Urchin Harakiri* with Bernard. I began my Introduction to this book with the following words:

> Bernard Bador's poetry to date is surely one of the most unique bodies of work to have been influenced by a range of French poetry that begins with Lautréamont, passes through Tzara and other Surrealist strategies of the 1920s and 30s and, for Bador, culminates in the poetry of St-John Perse. In the poetry of Bador, it is as if Perse's galleons of light and renewal (in an imaginary Caribbean devoid of repression and suffering) are suddenly sucked down into the still, black sheen of a petrified whirlpool. Bador's poetry evokes faceless lakes of still-being, grids of flashing lesions, and a garroted apocalypse resplendent with repugnant urges. There is an appetite for slivers here, and a special morbidity that recalls the sensibilities of the German poets Georg Trakl and Gottfried Benn (especially the Benn of the lugubrious and slashing *Morgue* poems, where one finds such images as mice building a nest in the belly of a little girl whose murdered corpse was left in a ditch).

Bernard Bador is not only of Hungarian ancestry but a descendent (we suspect) of the noble Bathory family, whose ancestors include the Countess Erzsebet Bathory (1560-1614), a one woman "death camp" who is on record as having tortured and slaughtered over 600 virgin peasants in order to renew her youth by bathing in their blood.

In Bador's poetry, I imagine that Erzsebet's unappeasible hunger for an eroticized mayhem has mysteriously come to rest, or let's say that it has subsided, like water might in a landscape, leaving the eroded shapes that make up his poetry. Such hunger has here taken on the form of static, compact stanzas that upon examination resemble plates of cold funeral meats. I imagine Erzsebet's psyche fluttering about these stanzas, nibbling and sipping, finding enough death to preoccupy and distract her from what might have been an endless, foodless flight through the Bathory/Bador progeny.

In June, 1986, Caryl Eshleman and I were invited to spend a month in Hungary by the Soros Foundation in NYC. The idea of the visit as well as contact with the Foundation came from our friend Gyula Kodolanyi whom we had met while he was a Fulbright Fellow at UC Santa Barbara in 1985. I went over some English versions of Gyula's poems with him (they had been done without his participation by people in England). By detailed questioning, asking Gyula to tell me (in his excellent English) exactly what the Hungarian word meant, and how it functioned in a line, I was able to ascertain whether the English translator had done accurate work or whether he had "improvised" upon the original.

In the course of several sessions, we moreorless rewrote 15 pages of Gyula's poetry and prose poetry. He began to read my own poetry, and by the end of the semester, our time with texts was divided between his work and my own. Gyula and I wanted to continue working together, and Gyula and his wife, Maria Illyes (the daughter of the poet, Gyula Illyes), who is a curator at the Museum of Fine Arts in Budapest, wanted us to visit Hungary.

The Soros Foundation paid our air fares and offered us a modest per diem that since we stayed with the Kodolanyis almost covered our land expenses. In exchange, they hoped that such a trip would result in some Hungarian writing finding its way into *Sulfur* magazine (which I had been editing since 1981). There was no plan at the point we arrived in Budapest. Gyula and I decided that we would work together 3 or 4 hours a day, 5 days a week, side by side, at his father-in-law's work table on the third floor of the Illyes home. Over this month we translated around 65 pages of Hungarian poetry, including work by Gyula, Miklós Radnóti, Miklós Mészöly, Ferenc Juhász, Sándor Csoóri, and Géza Szöcs. Such made up most of a Hungarian Section in *Sulfur* #21, 1988. For years I have wanted to translate more Hungarian poetry with Gyula but we have yet to figure out how to spend another month together (I would, in particular, like to do more Juhász).

I spent a little time in Czechoslovakia in 1976 and again in 1979. Other than what is left of the spectral power of Prague (the old Jewish cemetery there ought to be visited by every poet in the world), life in Czechoslovakia struck me as agonizingly monolithic grey. The fact that the poet Vladimir Holan had, between 1948 and 1963, gone out of his house twice, seemed symbolic of the cut-off between the life of the mind and the life of the state. During this period of time when his writing was unpublishable and his previous books unavailable, Holan looked at the walls within walls and spoke with Shakespeare, producing his poetic masterpiece "A Night with Hamlet," a 50 page poem which on its surface has nothing to do with the political surface of the 1950s, but whose depths, in massive oblique waves, contain the pessimism of a great world poet struggling against terrible odds to maintain a feel and respect for the human spirit.

For more information on Holan and his poem see the Note preceding the translation.

Antonin Artaud's "Revolt Against Poetry," one of the seminal recognitions of the extent to which all poets stand in belated relationship to poets of the past, was written in 1944, during one of his roughest times in the Rodez asylum.

"Pounding and Gism," and "Civil Status," co-translated with A. James Arnold, are revised dictations, of which there are seventy-three, in *Suppôts et suppliciations* (Gallimard, two volumes, 1978), the last book-length manuscript that Artaud himself edited. Along with these dictations, the book is made up of ten essays and thirty-five letters. For several months at the end of 1946, a secretary was hired to visit Artaud every morning at the Ivry clinic where he was living, to take down by hand material that he would dictate to her. In these days, Artaud would break into dictation at any moment—while in bed, at a cafe table, or with friends—only to interrupt himself and sink into a long silence. Luciane Abiet, the secretary, would arrive early in the morning, often while Artaud, still sleepy, would be sitting up in bed, his cafe au lait cooling on the bedside table. Abiet's difficulties in getting down exactly what Artaud said to her were compounded by the fact that he was missing all of his teeth and often fighting mental lacunae brought about by chloral hydrate or other drugs.

There is a note at the end of "Letter to André Breton" explaining the circumstances under which it was written. After the two pieces on Christ there is also a note.

I discovered "Dix ans que la langage est parti" ("Ten years that the language is gone") in Marc Dachy's magazine *Luna-Park #5* (1979). It is one of the few texts in which Artaud addresses the combination of writing and drawing on the same page, or as part of the same focus, that characterizes his notebooks since 1945 while in the Rodez museum (according to his devoted editor and literary executor, Paule Thévenin). Curiously, in this piece Artaud pinpoints the beginning of this dyadic practice in October 1939, when he would have been in the Ville-Evrard asylum, probably the low point of his life (he had been pronounced to be incurable and was held in the drug-addict ward). As far as I know, there are no notebooks from the Ville-Evrard period.

The Appendix revisits my apprentice-translator's relationship to Neruda's first two *Residencias en la tierra*. It will probably be of most interest to the young poet-translator. At the time I began to try my hand with translations of these poems I had no idea that I was taking hold of the tail of an international dragon that would subsequently pull me to Mexico, Japan, Peru and France. For the young poet, pervading all aspects of the poetic enterprise, translation opens up amazing vistas that, on one level, coalesce into the stunning sighting and command at the end of Rilke's "Archaic Torso of Apollo":

there is no place
that does not see you. You must change your life.

Notes

1. "Saving the Nuclear Bomb," by Wolfgang Giegerich, in *Facing Apocalypse*, Spring Publications, Dallas, 1987.

2. A. James Arnold's Introduction to *Lyric and Dramatic Poetry 1946-1982* contains a thoughtful commentary on Césaire's "late style," as found in I, *laminaria*.

Arthur Rimbaud:
The Drunken Boat

Pulled as I was down phlegmatic Rivers,
Suddenly—no longer a barge for towers!
Whooping Redskins with emptied quivers
Had nailed them naked to painted posts!

Contemptuous? Of every kind of crew:
Carriers of English cotton or Flemish wheat.
The moment my shrieking towers were subdued,
The Rivers let me plunge to open sea.

Amidst the furious slaps of racing tides,
I, last winter, blunter than children's brains,
I ran! No untied Peninsula's
Been trounced by a more triumphant din!

The tempest blessed my sea-born awakenings.
Lighter than cork, I skipped across rollers called
The eternal loop-the-loops of victims, ten nights,
Without missing the simpleton stares of lamps!

Sweeter than tart apple flesh to kids,
The green water probed my pine hull
And of the stains of blue wines and vomit
It scoured me, scattering rudder and grapnel.

From then on, I bathed in the Poem of the Sea,
Star-infused, lactescent, devouring
The verdant blue; where, ghastly and ravished
Flotsam, a rapt drowned man at times descends;

Where, tinting instantly the bluicities, deliriums
And slow rhythms under the day's rutilations,

Stronger than alcohol, vaster than our lyres,
The bitter russets of love ferment!

I know the sky split with lightning, and the undertows
And the currents and the waterspouts; I know the evening,
The Dawn as glorious as an entire nation of doves,
And I've seen sometimes what man thought he saw!

I've seen the sun low, spotted with mystic horrors,
Raying forth long violet coagulations,
Like actors in prehistoric plays the whitecaps
Flickering into the distance their shutter shudders!

I've dreamed of the green night with dazzled snows,
A kiss rising through the seas' eyes in slow motion,
The circulatory flow of outrageous saps,
And the bilious blue arousals of singer phosphors!

I've followed, for months on end, swells
Like exploding stables, battering the reefs,
Never dreaming that the Marys' luminescent feet
Could force a muzzle onto wheezing Oceans!

I've struck, are you aware, incredible Floridas
Comingling with flowers the eyes of panthers in the skins
Of men! Rainbows arched like bridle-reins
Below seas' horizons, taut to glaucous herds!

I've seen enormous swamps fermenting, weirs
Where in the reeds a whole Leviathan rots!
Cave-ins of water in the midst of standing calms,
The distances cataracting toward the abysses!

Glaciers, pearly waves, suns of silver, molten skies!
Hideous wrecks in the slime of fuscous gulfs
Where gigantic snakes devoured by bugs

Drop from twisted trees, squirting black perfumes!

I would've liked to show children these dorados
Of the blue wave, these gold, these singing fish.
—Flower foam cradled my berthless driftings
And at times I was winged by ineffable winds.

Sometimes, a martyr weary of poles and zones,
The very sea whose sobbing made my churning sweet
Proffered her yellow suckered shadow flowers
And I held there, like a woman on her knees...

Almost an island, tossing off my wales
The squabbles and dung of gossipy blond-eyed birds.
And so I scudded, while through my frayed
Cordage drowned sailors sank sleepwards, back first!

But now, a boat lost under the hair of coves,
Flung by the hurricane into birdless ether,
I whose carcass, drunk on water, no Monitor
Or Hanseatic schooner would've fished out;

Free, fuming, risen from violet mists,
I who pierced the reddening sky like a wall
Bearing exquisite jam for genuine poets—
Solar lichen and azure snot;

Who ran, speckled with electric lunules,
A crazy plank, by black sea horses escorted,
When the Julys with cudgel blows were crushing
The ultramarine skies into burning funnels;

I who trembled, hearing, at fifty leagues, the whimpers
Of Behemoth rutting and turgid Maelstroms,
Eternal spinner of blue immobilities,
I miss the Europe of age-worn parapets!

I've seen astral archipelagos! and isles
Whose raving skies open wide to the voyager:
—In those bottomless nights do you sleep, are you exiled,
A million golden birds, O Force of the future?—

But, truly, I've wept too much! Dawns are harrowing.
Each moon is atrocious, each sun bitter:
Acrid love has swollen me with inebriating torpors.
O let my keel burst! O let me be gone to the sea!

If there is one Europe I long for,
It's a chill, black puddle where, at the scented end of day,
A squatting child, utterly forlorn,
Releases a boat fragile as a butterfly in May.

No longer will I, bathed in your languors, O waves,
Slip into the wakes of cotton carriers,
Nor cut across the arrogance of flags and streamers,
Nor swim below the prison hulks' horrific stares.

{1871}

Pablo Neruda:
Thirteen Poems from
Residencia en la tierra I and II

Unity

There is something dense, united, settled in the depths,
repeating its number, its identical sign.
How one can tell that stones have touched time,
in their refined matter there is an odor of age,
of water that the sea brings, from salt and sleep.

I'm encircled by a single thing, a single movement:
a mineral weight, a honeyed light
cling to the sound of the word "noche":
the tint of wheat, of ivory, of tears,
things of leather, of wood, of wool,
archaic, faded, uniform,
collect around me like walls.

I work quietly, wheeling over myself,
a crow over death, a crow in mourning.
I mediate, isolated in the spread of seasons,
centric, encircled by a silent geometry:
a partial temperature drifts down from the sky,
a distant empire of confused unities
reunites encircling me.

Taste

From fake astrologies, from customs a bit lugubrious,
emptied into what is endless and always at hand,
I've retained a tendency, a taste for being alone.

From conversations as exhausted as old wood,
with the humility of chairs, with words occupied
in serving as slaves of secondary wills,
having a consistency of milk, from dead weeks,
from air chained above the cities.

Who can boast of a more solid patience?
Uncommon sense wraps me in a compact skin,
in a color reunited like a snake:
my creatures emerge from a deep repulsion,
ah, with a little alcohol I can say goodbye to this day
that I have chosen, equal among earthly days.

I live full of a common-colored stuff, silent
as an old mother, a patience fixed
as church shadow or the repose of bones.
I go full of those waters profoundly capable,
prepared, falling asleep with a sad stare.

Inside my guitar interior there's an old air,
dry and sonorous, permanent, immobile,
like a faithful nourishment, like smoke:
an element at rest, a living oil:
a bird of severity guards my head:
an immutable angel lives in my sword.

Single Gentleman

The young homosexuals and the horny girls,
the gaunt widows suffering from delirious insomnia,
the young wives pregnant thirty hours,
the raucous cats criss-crossing my garden in the dark—
like a necklace of throbbing sexual oysters
they encircle my solitary house
like enemies set up against my soul,
like conspirators in pajamas
exchanging countersigns of long thick kisses.

Radiant summer directs the lovers
in identical melancholy regiments
made up of fat, skinny, gay and sorrowful pairs:
under the elegant cocopalms, by the ocean and the moon,
there's a steady life of trousers and skirts,
a rustle of caressed silk stockings
and feminine breasts twinkling like eyes.

The petty employee, after a lot of bitching,
a week of boredom, the novels read in bed at night
has once and for all seduced his neighbor.
He escorts her to the wretched movies
where heroes are colts or impassioned princes,
and he fingers her sweet downy legs
with damp hot hands that stink of cigarettes.

The seducer's late afternoons and the nights of couples
join like double sheets to bury me,
and the hours after lunch when the male students,
the co-eds and the priests masturbate,
and animals openly hump,
and the bees smell of blood, and flies buzz angrily,

and cousins play peculiar games with their girl cousins,
and the doctors glare furiously at the husband of the young patient,
and the morning hours when the professor, absent-mindedly,
fulfills his conjugal duty and then sits down to breakfast,
and even more, the adulterers, who truly make love to each other
upon beds high and long as ocean liners:
securely, eternally, I am surrounded by
this great breathing forest entangled
with huge flowers like mouths and false teeth
and black roots shaped like fingernails and shoes.

Ritual of My Legs

For hours I've persistently watched my long legs
with my usual passion, with infinite curiosity and tenderness,
as if they had been the legs of a divine woman
thrust deep into the abyss of my thorax:
and the truth is, when time, when time passes
over the earth, over the roof, over my impure head,
and passes, time passes, and in my bed I do not feel at night
    that a woman is breathing, sleeping naked and at my side,
then strange, dark things take the place of the absent one,
vicious, melancholy thoughts
seed heavy possibilities in my bedroom,
and then, well, I watch my legs as if they had belonged to
    another body,
and vigorously and gently had been joined to my insides.

Like shoots or adorable feminine things,
from my knees they rise, cylindrical and dense,
a roily and compact stuff:
like the brutal, gross arms of a goddess,
like trees monstrously dressed as human beings,
like fatal, immense lips thirsty and quiet,
here is the best part of my body:
entirely substance, no complicated system
of feelings or windpipes or intestines or ganglia:
nothing but the pure, sweet weight of my own life,
nothing, but existing form and volume,
guarding life, however, in a complete way.

People walk the world today
hardly remembering they possess a body and in it life,
and there is fear, there is fear in the world of words that
    name the body,

and one speaks favorably of clothes,
it is possible to speak of pants, of suits,
of womens' underwear (of hose and garters for "señora"),
as if empty garments walked the streets
and a dark, obscene clothes closet had taken over the world.

Suits have existence, color, form, design,
and a profound place in our myths, too much of a place,
there's too much furniture, too many rooms in the world
and my body lives humbled between and under so many things,
obsessed with slavery and chains.

So, my knees, like knots,
particular, functional, evident,
neatly separate the halves of my legs:
actually, two different worlds, two different sexes
are not as different as these two halves.

From knee to foot, a hard form,
mineral, coldly useful, appears,
a creature of bone and persistence,
and the ankles are nothing but naked intention
exact and poised.

Without sensuality, short and hard, and masculine,
my calves are stocked
with muscular groups like complementary animals,
here too is life, subtle and acute,
without trembling it endures, waiting and acting.

In my ticklish feet,
as hard as the sun, and as open as flowers,
perpetual, magnificent soldiers
in the gray war of space,

everything ends, life definitely ends in my feet,
what is alien and hostile begins there:
names of the world, the frontier and what is remote,
the substantive and the adjectival I've no heart for
originate there with unrelenting density and coldness.

Always,
manufactured products, socks, shoes,
or simply infinite air
between my feet and the earth
intensifying what is isolated and solitary in my being,
something tenaciously inserted between my life and the earth,
something openly unfriendly and unconquerable.

Only Death

There are lonely cemeteries,
tombs full of bones with no sound,
the heart passing through a tunnel
blackness, blackness, blackness,
as if in a shipwreck we die inward,
as if drowning in our hearts,
as if falling from our skin to our soul.

There are cadavers,
there are feet of cold, clammy slabs,
there is death in the bones
like a pure sound,
like a bark with no dog,
wafting from certain bells, from certain tombs,
increasing in the humidity like weeping or rain.

I see, alone, at times,
coffins set sail
weighing anchor with pallid souls, women in dead tresses,
bakers white as angels,
pensive girls married to accountants,
coffins ascending the vertical river of the dead,
the royal purple river,
upward, sails swollen by the sound of death,
swollen by the silent sound of death.

To what is loud and clear death comes
like a shoe with no foot, a suit with no man,
comes knocking with a ring without stone or finger,
comes shrieking with no mouth, no tongue, no throat.
Yet its steps echo
and its clothing rustles, silent, like a tree.

I don't know, I know very little, I hardly see,
but I think its song is the color of moist violets,
of violets used to the earth,
for the face of death is green,
and the look of death is green,
with the prickly dampness of a violet leaf
and its solemn color of exasperated winter.

But death also moves through the world dressed as a broom,
licking the floor looking for souls,
death is in the broom,
is the tongue of death looking for the dead,
the needle of death looking for thread.

Death is in cots:
in sluggish mattresses, in black blankets
it lives stretched out, and suddenly blows:
it blows a dark sound that swells the sheets,
and there are beds sailing to a port
where death is waiting, dressed as an admiral.

"Walking Around"

It happens that I am tired of being a man.
It happens that I enter tailorshops and movies
shriveled, numb, like a felt swan
circling a pond of origin and ash.

The smell of barbershops makes me howl.
All I want is a respite from stones and from wool,
all I want is to see no establishments, no gardens,
no merchandise, no eyeglasses, no elevators.

It happens that I am tired of my feet and my fingernails,
and my hair and my shadow.
It happens that I am tired of being a man.

Still it would be delicious
to scare an accountant with a cut lily,
or to kill a nun with a blow to the ear.
It would be beautiful
to sidle through the streets with an obscene knife
yelling until I froze to death.

I don't want to go on being a root in the dark,
vacilating, extended, shivering with sleep,
downward, in the moist guts of the earth,
absorbing and thinking, eating everyday.

I don't want all all these afflictions.
I don't want to continue being root and tomb,
solely underground, a bodega of corpses,
frozen stiff, dying from anguish.

That's why Monday blazes like gasoline
when it sees me coming with my jailbird face,

and it yowls in passing like a wounded wheel,
taking steps of hot blood into the night.

And it shoves me into certain corners, into certain humid houses,
into hospitals where bones jut from the window,
into certain shoestores that smell of vinegar,
into streets frightening as fissures.

There are sulphur-colored birds and horrible intestines
hanging from the doors of houses that I hate,
there are false teeth forgotten in a coffeepot,
there are mirrors
that should have wept from shame and terror,
there are umbrellas everywhere, and poison, and navels.

I walk along calmly, with eyes, with shoes,
with fury, completely out of it,
I pass, I cross offices and orthopedic shops,
and courtyards where washing is hanging from a wire:
underwear, towels and shirts that weep
sluggish splotchy tears.

Melancholy in the Families

I keep a blue vial,
inside it an ear and a portrait:
when night binds
the owl's feathers,
when the harsh cherry tree
shatters its labia and threatens
with husks often perforated by the ocean wind,
I know there are great sunken wastes,
quartz in ingots,
muck,
waters blue for a battle,
much silence, many
veins running backwards and camphors,
fallen things, medals, tenderness,
parachutes, kisses.

It is no more than a step from one day to another,
a lone bottle skipping across the sea,
and a dining room where roses arrive,
a dining room as abandoned as a fishbone: I refer to
a shattered wine glass, a curtain, to the depths of
a deserted room through which a river passes
dragging rocks. A house
settled into the origin of rain,
a two-storied house with compulsory windows,
entangled with faithful vines.

I visit in the evening, I arrive
full of mud and death,
dragging the earth and its roots,
its errant belly where cadavers
sleep with wheat,
metals, felled elephants.

But above all there's a terrible,
terrible abandoned dining room
with broken cruets
and vinegar running under the chairs,
an arrested moon ray,
something dark, and I search for a comparison within:
perhaps it is a store encircled by the sea,
its torn cloths dripping brine.
It is only an abandoned dining room,
around it there are wastes,
sunken factories, boards
that I alone know,
because I am sad and old,
and know the earth, and am sad.

Ode with a Lament

Oh girl among roses, oh pressure of doves,
oh garrison of fish and rosebushes,
your soul is a bottle full of thirsty salt
and a bell full of grapes is your skin.

I have nothing, alas, to give you but fingernails
or eyelashes or molten pianos,
or dreams frothing from my heart,
dust dreams racing like black horsemen,
dreams full of velocity and misfortune.

Looking at ash-colored horses and yellow dogs,
I can only love you with poppies and kisses,
with garlands drenched by the rain.
I can only love you with waves at my back,
between vague blows of sulphur and brooding water,
swimming against the cemeteries flowing down certain rivers
with wet fodder growing over the sad plaster tombs,
swimming across submerged hearts
and the pallid birth certificates of dug-up children.

There is so much death, so many funerals
in my abandoned passions, my desolate kisses,
there is a water falling on my head,
while my hair grows,
a water like time, a liberated black water
with a nocturnal voice, with a cry
of birds in the rain, with an interminable
shadow of damp wings protecting my bones:
while I dress, while
interminably I stare at mirrors, at windowpanes,
I hear someone pursue me calling me
sobbing in a voice rotted by time.

You are standing on the earth, full
of lightning and teeth.
You spread kisses and murder ants.
You weep from health, from onions, from bees,
from a burning alphabet.
You are like a blue and green sword
and undulate to my touch like a river.

Come to my soul dressed in white, with a bunch
of blood-smeared roses, and goblets of ashes,
come with an apple and a horse
for here there is a dark parlour, a broken candelabrum,
some warped chairs waiting for winter,
and a pigeon dead, with a number.

Nuptial Material

Erect like a cherry tree without bark or blossoms,
particular, ignited, with saliva and veins,
and fingers, and testicles,
I watch a girl of paper and moon,
horizontal, trembling and breathing and white,
and her nipples like two separate codes,
and the rosebush uniting her thighs where
her vulva of nocturnal eyelashes winks.

Pallid, overflowing,
I feel words submerge in my mouth,
words like drowned children,
and onward and onward and ships sprouting teeth,
and waters and latitude like burned forests.

I'll arrange her like a sword or a mirror,
and I'll open her timorous legs until I die,
and I'll bite her ears and her veins,
and I'll make her retreat with eyes closed
in a river dense with green semen.

I will inundate her with poppies and lightning bolts,
will truss her in knees, in lips, in needles,
will enter her with inches of bawling epidermis,
with criminal pressure and soaked hair.

I'll make her flee escaping through fingernails and gasps
toward never, toward nothing,
climbing up viscous marrow and oxygen,
clutching memories and reasons
like a single hand, like a severed finger
brandishing a fingernail of helpless salt.

She must run sleeping down roads of skin
in a country of ashen gum and ashes,
fighting with knives, and bedsheets, and ants,
and with eyes that fall upon her like corpses,
and with drops of black matter slithering
like blind fish or bullets of jelled water.

Sexual Water

Tumbling in big solitary drops,
in tooth-like drops,
in big thick drops of marmalade and blood,
tumbling in big drops,
the water falls,
like a sword in drops,
like a ripping river of glass,
falls biting,
striking the axis of symmetry, sticking to the soul's seams,
breaking abandoned things, saturating the darkness.

It is only a breath, more humid than sobs,
a liquid, a sweat, a nameless oil,
a sharp movement,
forming, thickening,
the water falls,
in big slow drops,
towards its sea, towards its dry ocean,
towards its waterless wave.

I see a spacious summer, a death rattle leaving a granary,
bodegas, cicadas,
thronging masses, stimulants,
bedrooms, girls
sleeping with their hands upon their hearts,
dreaming of bandits, of conflagrations,
I see ships,
I see trees of marrow
bristling like rabid cats,
I see blood, daggers and women's hose,
and men's hair,
I see beds, see corridors where a virgin shrieks,
I see blankets and organs and hotels.

I see the stealthy dreams,
I admit the final days,
also the origins, also the memories,
like an eyelid horrendously raised by force
I am looking.

And then there is this sound:
a red noise of bones,
meat fastening to meat,
and yellow legs like conjoining ears of corn.
I listen in the crossfire of kisses,
listen, jolted between gasps and wails.
I am watching, hearing,
with half my soul at sea and half my soul on land,
and with both halves of my soul I watch the world.

And although it closes my eyes and utterly covers my heart,
I see a deaf water fall,
in big deaf drops.
Like a hurricane of gelatin,
like a cataract of jellyfish and sperm.
I see a turbid rainbow flow.
I see its waters crossing at the bone.

Ode to Federico García Lorca

If I could cry from fear in a lonely house,
if I could gouge out my eyes and devour them,
I would do it for your voice of mournful orange trees
and for your poetry that rings out in shouts.

For you they paint hospitals blue,
schools and maritime quarters are born,
wounded angels are covered with feathers,
nuptial fish are plated with scales,
sea urchins go flying into the sky:
for you tailorshops with their black membranes
fill with ladles and blood,
they swallow red ribbons, kill each other with kisses
and dress up in white.

When you fly disguised as a peach,
when you laugh the laugh of hurricaned rice,
when to sing you rattle the arteries, the teeth,
the throat and the fingers,
I would die for the sweetness that you are,
I would die for the red lakes
where in the midst of autumn you live
with a fallen charger and a blood-covered god,
I would die for the cemeteries that
like ashen rivers pass at night, between submerged bells:
rivers dense as dormitories of sick soldiers,
that suddenly swell
toward death in rivers with marble numbers,
rotted crowns and funeral ointments:
I would die to see you at night
watching the drowned crosses swing by,
standing there, and crying,
before the river of death you cry

abandonedly, woundedly,
you sob sobbing, your eyes filled
with tears, with tears, with tears.

If I could, at night, completely alone and lost,
collect the oblivion, the shadows, the smoke
over railroads and steamships,
with a black funnel,
biting the ashes,
I would do it for the tree in which you burgeon,
for the nests of golden water you assemble,
for the vinework covering your bones
communicating to you the secret of night.

Cities smelling of wet onions
wait for you to pass singing hoarsely,
silent sperm ships pursue you,
green swallows nest in your hair
along with snails and weeks—
volute masts and cherry trees
circulate for sure at the sight of
your pale head with fifteen eyes,
your mouth of submerged blood.

If I could pack the mayors' offices with soot
and, sobbing, knock over the clocks,
then I might witness broken-lipped summer
arrive at your house, multitudes
arriving in agonized clothing,
regions of sad grandeur arriving,
dead plows and poppies arriving,
gravediggers and jockeys arriving,
planets and maps with blood arriving,
divers covered with ashes arriving,
masked men dragging maidens
pierced by huge knives arriving,

roots, veins, hospitals,

spring water, ants,

the night arrives with a bed on which

a solitary hussar dies among spiders,

a rose of hatred and a handful of pins arrive,

a hazy yellow vessel arrives,

a child borne by a windy day arrives,

and I arrive with Oliverio, Norah,

Vicente Aleixandre, Delia,

Maruca, Malva Marina, María Luisa and Larco,

the Blonde, Rafael Ugarte,

Cotapos, Rafael Alberti,

Carlos, Bebé, Manolo Altolaguirre,

Molinari,

Rosales, Concha Méndez,

and others who don't come to mind.

Come that I may crown you, a youth of health

and butterflies, a youth pure

as black lightning perpetually free—

just between us, now,

when no one's left among the rocks,

let's speak simply, eye to eye:

what does poetry serve if not the dew?

What does poetry serve if not that night

when an acrid dagger finds us, that day,

that dusk, that broken corner

where the violated heart of man prepares to die?

Above all at night,

at night there are many stars,

all of them within a river

like a ribbon next to the windows

of houses filled with the poor.

Someone among them has died, maybe
they've lost their job in the offices,
in the hospitals, in the elevators,
in the mines,
beings suffer stubbornly wounded
and there is purpose and weeping everywhere:
while the stars flow in an unending river
there's much weeping at the windows,
thresholds are worn away by weeping,
bedrooms are soaked with weeping
that arrives as a wave biting the carpets.

Federico,
you see the world, the streets,
the vinegar,
the farewells at the station
when smoke lifts its decisive wheels
toward where there is nothing but
separations, stones, railroad tracks.

So many people everywhere asking questions.
There is the blindman covered with blood, the enraged,
the broken-hearted,
and the wretch, a tree of fingernails,
the bandit with his backpack of envy.

Such is life, Federico, here you have
the things my friendship can offer you,
the friendship of a melancholy virile male.
On your own you've learned many things,
you will come to know other things, slowly.

Autumn Returns

A mourningcast day drifts from the bells
like a fluttering, vague widow veil,
it is a color, a dream
of cherries sunk in the earth,
it is a smoke tail that comes without consolation
changing the color of the water and of the kisses.

I don't know if I make myself understood: when from the heights
night approaches, when the poet alone
at the window hears the autumn charger galloping,
when the leaves of trampled fear crackle in his arteries,
there is something over the sky, like burly ox
tongue, something in the doubt of the sky and of the atmosphere.

Things return to their places,
the indispensable lawyer, the hands, the oil,
the bottles,
all the indications of life: beds especially
are filled with a bloody liquid,
people confide in sordid ears,
assassins clamber down stairs,
yet it is not this, but the old gallop,
the horse of the old autumn trembling, persisting.

The horse of the old autumn has a red beard,
a lather of fear covers its cheeks
and the air following it is shaped like an ocean
and the perfume of drifting buried decay.

Every day there descends from the sky an ashen color
that pigeons must spread over the earth:
a cord woven by oblivion and tears,
time that has slept long years inside bells,

everything,
old threadbare suits, women who see snow coming,
black poppies that no one can contemplate without dying,
everything falls into the hands I raise
in the midst of the rain.

There is No Forgetting (Sonata)

If you ask me where I have been
I have to say "It happens."
I have to speak of ground darkened by stones,
of the river that enduring destroys itself:
I know only the things that birds lose,
the sea left behind, or my tearful sister.
Why so many regions, why does one day
attach to another? Why does a black night
accumulate in one's mouth? Why the dead?

If you ask me from where I come, I have to converse with
    broken things,
with deeply-embittered utensils,
with great beasts often rotted
and with my own anguished heart.

Those who have passed are not remembered
nor is the yellowish dove, asleep in oblivion,
nor the faces with tears,
the fingers at throats,
nor that which tumbles from the leaves:
the obscurity of an elapsed day,
a day nourished with our sad blood.

Here are some violets, swallows,
everything that pleases us and appears
on saccharine cards in long gowns
around which time and sweetness stroll.

But we must not penetrate beyond those teeth,
must not bite into the husks amassed by silence,
for I do not know what to answer:
there are so many dead,

and so many sea walls cracked by the red sun,
and so many heads smashed against boats,
and so many hands that have locked up kisses,
and so many things that I want to forget.

José Hierro:
Two Poems

Fe De Vida

I know winter's here,
behind this door. Know
if I went out now
I'd find everything dead,
struggling to be reborn.
Know if I look for a branch
I won't find it.
Know if I look for a hand
to free me of oblivion
I won't find it.
Know if I look for what's gone
I won't find it.

But here, I am. I move,
live. Am called José
Hierro. Joy. (Joy
that this fell at my feet.)
Nothing in order. Everything bust,
about to not be.

But I feel joy
for while everything's dead
I'm still alive and I know it.

Wherever you are, and how
I'll find you, sombra, sombra,
sombra...
          You broke rocks down,
shaped them with sun
with tristeza. I knew
I made a secret there
of peace, a heart
beating for me.

That you would be, sombra,
sombra, sombra; that name
that form, and that life
would be, sombra. As if
you couldn't be life.
have form, have name.

Sombra: under the rocks,
under such silence
—hardness and light,
gold and grass—that, who
solicits me, who
speaks to me, how
grasp it... (I dont find
the keys)... Sombra, sombra,
sombra... How grasp it
and let it go...

          Suddenly,
dazzlingly,
water shapes
a diamond. A
revelation...
          Azul:
in the azure it was

in the celestial pyre
in the pulp of day
the key. Now I remember:
I'd gone back to Italy. *Azul*
azul, azul: this was
the word (not *sombra,*
sombra, sombra). I remember
now—how clear—
what's continued to sound
unsuspected. I've gone back
to Italy, to the adventure
of serenity,
of beauty, grace,
proportion...

      By these
plazas the sun strips
each morning, the soul
sailed, clean
and blazing. But tell me,
azul (or am I speaking to sombra?),
what dimension do you lend
this hour of mine; who
tore away the wings
of life. And who I was
I don't know. Who he
was lived instants
I remember now.
What soul of mine, in what body
not mine, walked
this way, winding
love, between surges
of rock, between surges
flaring (waves

burst assaulting
towering cliffs)...

Between surges... Waves...
Gray... Waves... Sombra... I've turned
to forget the revealing
word. Beaches...
Waves... Sombra... Had something
of harmony, a place
where I am... (Sombra, sombra,
sombra)... where I am not.
No; the word was not
sombra. The shine of the sky,
the rose rock, have returned
to their silence. Are
before me. I study them
and immediately
they are gone. The equilibrium,
harmony, grace
are gone. Now sombra, sombra
(and so clear).

Who dissipated the place
(or time) that gave me
its blood that secreted
the time (or place)
did not live. And so
I remember what
had lived in my body
and soul. Which makes
here, in my memory,
this busted plane, old
Junker, under December's
moon. The mist,
the frost, that road
unto silence, that

sea was announcing
this very instant
isn't mine either.
Who knows what was said by
the waves of this rock.
who knows what
—before— this rock might have said
if I had hit upon
the right word to dissolve it
into the future. Such was
—yesterday— the word
unspoken. Such is
the word today
has been pronounced,
has burned in its pronouncement,
has been lost
for good.

César Vallejo:
Four Prose Poems

The Need to Die

Gentlemen:

It pleases me to inform you, by means of these lines, that death, more than a punishment, penalty or limitation imposed on man, is a necessity, the most imperative and irrevocable of all human necessities. Our need to die surpasses our need to be born and to live. We could do without being born but we could not do without dying. Until now no one has said: "1 have a need to be born." However, one frequently does say: "I have a need to die." On the other hand, to be born is, so it seems, very easy, since no one has ever said that it was very difficult for him and that he put forth a lot of effort to enter this world; whereas dying is more difficult than one thinks. This proves that the need to die is enormous and irresistible, since it is well known that the more difficult it is to satisfy a necessity the larger it looms. One yearns more for that which is less accessible.

If someone were to write to another always telling him that his mother continued to enjoy good health, the recipient would end up feeling a mysterious discomfort, not really thinking that he was being lied to and that most likely his mother must have died, but under the weight of the subtle and tacit need overwhelming him that his mother ought to die. This person would make the respective calculations and think to himself: "This cannot be. It's impossible that my mother is not already dead." In the end he will feel an anguished need to know that his mother has died. Otherwise, he will end up accepting it as a fact.

An ancient Islamic legend recounts that a son reached his three hundredth year among a people for whom life ended at the most at fifty. While in exile, the son, in his two hundreth year, asked about his father and was told: "He's in good health." But when, fifty years later, he returned to his town and learned that the author of his days had died two hundred years ago, he seemed tranquil, murmuring: "I have known this for many years." Of course. The son's need for the father to die had been for him, in its hour, irrevocable, fatal and had been fatally fulfilled also in its hour, in reality.

Rubén Dario has said that the sorrow of the gods lies in not reaching death. As for men, if, from the moment they are conscious, they could be sure of reaching death, they would be happy forever. But unfortunately, men are never sure of dying: they feel an obscure desire and a yearning to die, but they always doubt that they will die. The sorrow of men, we declare, lies in never being certain of death.

{Paris, 1926}

The three hundred womanly states of the Eiffel Tower are frozen. The Hertzian cultural mane of the tower, its downy sights, its vivid steelwork, bolted to a moral Cartesian system, are frozen.

The Bois de Boulogne, green from private clause, is frozen.

The Chamber of Deputies, where Briand cries out: "I hearby call on all the peoples of the earth...," and at whose doors the guard unconsciously caresses his cartridge of human uneasiness, his simple manly bomb, his eternal Pascalian principle, is frozen.

The Champs-Elysées, gray from public clause, is frozen.

The statues that periplanate the Place de Concord and above whose Phrygian caps time can be heard studying to be infinite are frozen.

The dice of the Parisian Catholic Calvaries are frozen even on the face of the threes.

Astonished on the Gothic needles of Notre-Dame and Sacré-Coeur, the civil cocks are frozen.

The maiden of the Parisian countryside, whose thumb never repeats itself while measuring the range of her eyes, is frozen.

The bidirectional andante of Stravinsky's "The Firebird" is frozen.

On the Richelieu amphitheater blackboard of the Sorbonne Einstein's scribblings are frozen.

The airplane tickets for the flight from Paris to Buenos Aires—two hours, 23 minutes, 8 seconds—are frozen.

The sun is frozen.

The fire at the center of the earth is frozen.

The meridian father and the parallel son are frozen.

The two deviations of history are frozen.

My manly minor act is frozen.

My sexual oscillation is frozen.

{Paris, in the late 1920s}

The Footfalls of a Great Criminal

When they turned off the lights, I felt like laughing. Things renewed their labors in the dark, at the point where they had been stopped; in a face, the eyes lowered to the nasal shells and took an inventory of certain missing optical powers, retrieving them one by one; a naval scale imperiously summoned the scales of a fish; three parallel rain drops halted at the height of a lintel, awaiting another drop that doesn't know why it had been delayed; the policeman on the corner blew his nose noisily, emphasizing in particular his left nostril; the highest and the lowest steps of a spiral staircase began to make signs to each other that alluded to the last passer-by to climb them. Things, in the dark, renewed their labors, animated by an uninhibited happiness, conducting themselves like people at a great ceremonial banquet, where the lights went out and all remained in the dark.

When they turned off the light, a better distribution of boundaries and frames was carried out around the world. Each rhythm was its own music; each needle of a scale moved as little as a destiny could move, that is to say, until nearly acquiring an absolute presence. In general, a delightful game was created between things, one of liberation and justice. I watched them and grew content, since in myself as well the grace of the numeral dark curvetted.

I don't know who let there be light again. The world began to crouch once more in its shabby pelts: the yellow one of Sunday, the ashen one of Monday, the humid one of Tuesday, the judicious one of Wednesday, sharkskin for Thursday, a sad one for Friday, a tattered one for Saturday. Thus the world reappeared, quiet, sleeping, or pretending to sleep. A hair-raising spider with three broken legs emerged from Saturday's sleeve.

{Paris, 1926}

The Conflict between the Eyes and the Gaze

Often I have seen things that others have also seen. This inspires me with a subtle, tiptoeing anger, into whose intimate presence blood flows from my solitary flanks.

—The sun has broken through, —I say to a man.

And he's responded to me:

—Yes. A sweet, fallow sun.

I had felt that the sun truly is sweet and fallow. So I want to ask another man what he knows about this sun. He confirmed my impression and this confirmation hurts me, a vague hurt that digs in under my ribs. Is it not then certain that I was facing the sun as it broke through? And, this being the case, that man had emerged as from a side mirror, without risking anything, to murmur at my side: "Yes, a sweet, fallow sun." An adjective stands out on each side of my temples. No, I will ask another man about this sun. The first one had lied or joked as if to supplant me.

—The sun has broken through, —I say to another man.

—Yes, very overcast, —he responds.

Later still, I've said to another:

—The sun has broken through.

And this one argues:

—An incomplete sun.

Where can I go where there will be no side mirror, whose surface faces me head on, no matter how much I advance sideways and look straight ahead!

Beautiful absurdities appear alongside a man and disappear, an urgent agile steed, requiring a halter, number, and rider. But men love to bridle for love of the rider and not for love of the animal. I have to bridle, if only for love of the animal. And no one will feel what I feel. And no one will have the power now to supplant me.

{Paris, 1926}

André Breton:
A Man and a Woman
Absolutely White

In the depths of the parasol I see the marvelous prostitutes.
Their dresses faded beside the streetlamp the color of the woods.
They take a big piece of wallpaper out with them for a walk.
One you cannot look at without heartache over the demolition of
     ancient floors.
Or else a white marble shell fallen from a mantel.
Or else a filament of their necklaces that blur in the mirrors behind them
A powerful instinct for combustion seizes the streets where they wait
Like singed flowers.
Their eyes raising in the distance a wind of stone.
While they remain engulfed and motionless at the whirlpool's center
For me nothing can equal the significance of their careless thoughts
The fresh gutter water in which their little boots steep the shadows
     of their beaks
The reality of those fistfuls of cut hay into which they disappear.
I see their breasts put a dot of sun into the deep night
and the time these take to fall and to rise is the only exact measure of life
I see their breasts which are stars over the waves.
Their breasts in which the invisible blue milk sobs forever.

Aimé Césaire:
Three Poems

Lynch I

Why does the spring grab me by the throat? what does it want of me? so what even if it does not have enough spears and military flags? I jeer at you spring for flaunting your blind eye and your bad breath. Your stupration your infamous kisses. Your peacock tail makes tables turn with patches of jungle (fanfares of saps in motion) but my liver is more acidic and my venefice stronger than your malefice. The lynch it's 6 PM in the mud of the bayou it's a black handkerchief fluttering at the top of the pirate ship mast it's the strangulation point of a fingernail up to the carmine of an interjection it's the pampa it's the queen's ballet it's the sagacity of science it's the unforgettable copulation. O lynch salt mercury and antimony! The lynch is the blue smile of a dragon enemy of angels the lynch is an orchid too lovely to bear fruit the lynch is an entry into matter the lynch is the hand of the wind bloodying a forest whose trees are galls brandishing in their hand the smoking torch of their castrated phallus, the lynch is a hand sprinkled with the dust of precious stones, the lynch is a release of hummingbirds, the lynch is a lapse, the lynch is a trumpet blast a broken gramophone record a cyclone's tail its train lifted by the pink beaks of predatory birds. The lynch is a gorgeous shock of hair that fear flings into my face the lynch is a temple crumbled and gripped by the roots of a virgin forest. O lynch lovable companion beautiful squirted eye huge mouth mute save when an impulse spreads there the delirium of glanders weave well, lightningbolt, on your loom a continent bursting into islands an oracle contortedly slithering like a scolopendra a moon setting in the breach the sulfur peacock ascending in the summary loophole of my assassinated hearing.

Laughable

Letter to a far-away friend

I have not been nailed to the most absurd of rocks
No winged exploit has ever visited me
Out of the abyss no chorus rises toward me
Except at times the hiccup of shipwrecked cargo
No use mentioning
That I don't give a damn about civil status
established obviously from mere nostalgia
I have not been slashed by some obliging beak
Threatened with some serious retaliation
other than that
The difficulties with hindsight
being largely compensated by the broadening of sight
I do not graze on panic
I do not ruminate remorse
All I do is peck about the ordinary season
On the lookout during a brief flash
(that time called dead)
for the wake of a lost acquiescence
or if you prefer of an injunction

PS:
But given that all vigor has vanished
That the tide withdraws
That the tradewind is dying on me
That even pollen and sand fail to reach me
natal
That between myself and myself
the futile track startles and turns on itself
Let my silence alone deposit
With one swoop into the hollow of my recumbence
The ill-deciphered jubilation of a
solitary magma
Horseman of time and sea foam

from Configurations

Nothing ever delivers but the opacity of words

Words of decency and indecency
Words of harsh remarks

Coiling of the great thirst of being
spiral of the great urge and of the great return of being
knot of algae and entrails
knot of the rising and of the ebbing of being.
I almost forgot: words as well for the slack:
it is knotted the rage of not saying.

Torpor does not speak.
Thick. Heavy. Gross.
A precipitate. Who dared?
the quicksanding is at the limit.
At the limit of the muck.
ah!
     there's no speech but in outburst.
     To smash the muck.
       to smash.

Diction of a delirium binding the entire universe
to the surrection of a rock!

Bernard Bador:

Ten Poems from
Sea Urchin Harakiri

Essence

In the frondescence
of waking
blued by secret meathooks
sleep
holds vigil over lightning
spiraling between platinum naves.

Cripples
toss and turn
in the quicksand
off stage
where inert pulsations
are read upside down.

At the detour of alerts
shouted on the sickly
orbit
of fleeing upheavals
origin
ends.

The Transparent Man

In the recessed tomb of eyelids
the recumbent statue honks the crucified's horn.

The eyes deflate, saturated with beaks
concretized by the cold.

Inside the cage, space pleats, unfurls,
then shreds under the claws of roots.

Before your very eyes the sky swells expanding
gigantically to swallow the Niagara of the dead.

Evil Port

Night disembowels itself on the rocks,
a hideous wrackish mud is filling your mouth,
the sand is choking in your heart of hearts.

All has fled—except the soul slag
dangling from the gluey harbor's crane,
mist of visages in dry-dock, beakful of bearded owls.

"Journey to the End of Night"

Man gnaws his eyes, his blood and his bowels
before a tiny pile of fat, eczematous
pennies which pustulate in his hide of
a goatskin bag tanned with gold.

A bronze liberty kicks him in the ass,
blows of terrible hunger satiated
in garbage cans where the light itself
is rotting. And his dreams give off

rancidity like gravel buttered on thick
slices of bread in the harbor of dragging
fog on the mutilated sea of prosperous
cargos. The acne of mobs, disemployed

from life, suppurates on the stars of
washed-out decals of a sealed mass grave.
A cosmic anal filth coruscates
hemorrhoidal light on the rubble orbit

of copulating vermin. And the sun,
too handsome to soil himself in this miasma,
unloads his lead clots into sewers
overflowing with the aborted.

To hell with these scrap soul
merchants, these hucksters of blood!
But the nerves are already forging
their cavalry in the future ghettos.

The Hand

A wall of flies
advances across the pulpy sores
of gravediggers
on a pilgrimage to the sources.

On the altar,
where the bones are smoldering,
a hand gloved in gold
paws the Cabalistic dust
in order to strangle the numbers.

Odyssey

to Saint-John Perse

A powerful sea of lemons
is lifting
over the firing-squads
green clouds
of empty thrones.

Your lips tumefied
with incense bites swell
at the blast of hunting horns
in deconsecrated churches'
luminous coal.

Don't you hear
the burned forests being hunted down
on the forbidden trails
of the exoduses
of your cemetery-tied hands?

With pubis blows
set in a cloud of fever
one must fell
the perfumed lianas
of black religions.

Suddenly
the corsair's keel
crashes into the carcass
of drums abandoned
in the cannon-enclosed wind.

At precisely the foam of lies
I will nail up
the exasperated

tunnel sun
in which you lie in agony.

Have you not seen the legions of angels
falling
like beribboned locusts
over the pyramids of alphabets
as they drift toward Cygnus?

On every side
of the soft octopi
marching toward echoing depths
ramparts check
the droughts' assault.

In flabby silences
that absence alone troubles
every voice
skewered by lunar blades
shreds.

Higher
the sacrificed gaze of the goldsmith
has polished
the insane battle-
encrusted mirror.

In the snow of calendars
buried
under gentians
the chamois-
yellow vessel has sunk.

The thirst of fetishes
carved
into the curare of anguish

is choking
in thick African furs.

In your flesh of steppes
let the nomad
sculpt the amphore
into which cavalcades of powerful
four-in-hands are poured.

Under the reign of huge rose windows
submit yourself
to the invasions of gargoyles brocaded
with the flags of pungent winds
from Bactriane.

On the backside of druidic mistletoe
contemplate
the milky armfuls
of meditations
of soaring rock forests.

On your jet-black hair
vast migrations of hours
are spreading over
the brilliance of royal favors
on the tattoos of slaves.

Caravans
move out
in the blue rose of dawn
toward saffron landscapes beyond
the gypsum found in fathomless eagles' throats.

After the exile of the ants
you follow
the putrid hyena flesh

as far as the pestilence
in which shadows graze.

Don't you hear
the dance of grimaces
on the bare walls of your fears
sacrifice your pride
to the waking of menhirs?

A gigantic avalanche of silence
crushes
space into a fleeing expansion of
blue atoms, hard and cold
stellar seeds.

Birth

Camels pregnant
with flies searching for facetted
fissures.

O forger wells
of bones gone to seed!

High priests
initiated into impotency
pack up the graffiti of C.O.D.
liturgies.

Better to make a hole in the air
than at a blind intersection
to core the bulbs of the Cross.

Acrid,
a spar of rose wreckage skims the second,
a wound of light
on the faded mandala of eyes in ashes.

Behind all this,
a long mauve cry is escaping,
its high note has sliced the petrified biruti.

Stillborn, flies
are swarming
the skin of veiled Vestals.

Soul
hookable
wall.

Progress

Jacaranda blindings
heightened by summer's ponderous cymbals.

The melody slinks off to die
under a rolling-mill of potato bugs,
ardent myosoti spouses.

Under the flashings,
faceless sucklings
are flaying the dancers.

The turbulent macaw mutism
is quartered on a wheel of main-jibs
swollen with bear bites.

Tristan Tzara tramples the sacred wells
of the peacock butterflies
scythed by shamrock machetes.

At the call of the termite totems,
pastel blue moray eels
begin to lay tides,
popping sleigh-bells
under the murmuring of heraldic sables.

Ah charisma of deluges!
Hand-to-hand of turgescent mud
into which asphyxiated
walruses are plunging their tusks.

A Cape of Wild Flies

Beyond the silent aurochs-haunted forests,
victims give birth to victims,
white she-wolf jaws crush
the black lord's

epileptic sleigh on the powdery
sand of summer, sand
promised to the horse-blood drinkers.
The multiple odyssey under each step!

A hardened rainbow shelters the tarot players
whose fauve oil faces long to crush
the trembling she-mummies
scratching at the surfaceless sheer walls.

Bloodsplashed palettes of eyes.
The fine nerves we entangle in concrete clouds.
After all, the moon does
menstruate on the shadows of our limp

members and bonzai willows dot
the weary fur of our retinas.
Her eyelids hung with deadly nightshade
stuffed bats, her sheets

wet with the blood of virgins,
the royal harpy again and again
yields to the peaty crusades of orgasms.
The juice of marine snails

germinated on Uranus streams
from the sex of icy stones

while witches from the Karpaths
anoint the Countess's vaginal chasm.

In the darkness of underground wash houses,
hordes of infuriated, trilobite-fringed
fledglings immerse themselves in the storm graffiti
chiseled in our limestone lungs.

Curdled Skulls

The butcher debones the violets
with a suckling's love
for the alpine breast
scattered with curdled skulls

    *

At the sprouting of the first bud
a blue shriek of saws
which the madness of the rake would have liked
to twist around its little prongs

    *

Sound attacked from every side,
codfish rotting in the beds of bishops
mossy with canonical butts

    *

In the flower bed
a slug is urinating on a masochistic spider

    *

Obese women with very delicate joints
dragging about bloated snarling cats
packed with porcupine quills

    *

Tongues vibrating
in the tops of bald trees

fish shadows teeming
with schools of men

*

Out of breath but smooth with semen
milky spiders
forage in our troubled eyes

*

The bird comes into you through your eyes
ripping out in beakfuls
the tender shoots of your steps

*

Sounds shelled on a rosary of barbed wire

*

Onto the night of curdled eyes
caterpillars
lay
the droppings of our orphan cries

*

Choked under the mourning caramel
mobs bury themselves
with velvety yells

*

Covered with antique snow
the pollen of our draw-bridge languages

*

Music hanged itself
from a tumefied tongue—
in search of the echo
a fly paces up and down

*

An orchestra conductor in tears
elevates to fire's limits
the lacquered veins of luminous winds

*

The sun longs for gravedigging waves
but shivers at the sweet swift swish
of the multicolored harp of razors

*

A capillary breath
marinated in embrace's smut
irrigates
the aurora of the living disguised as the UnDead

Miklós Radnóti:
Six Poems

Anxiously Autumn Arrives

Out of enraged, iron-colored flags
the sun whirls anxiously, belching vapor
—and the light flitting away
bites into plummeting fog.

Disheveled clouds, the sky mirror
rippled by wind. Blue streaks off.
A swallow in low swoops
ready to depart writes a shrieking note.

Anxiously autumn arrives.
Rust lifts and sinks on the foliage.
Heavenly breath is cool.
The sky, coldly, merely smokes—
the sun now no more potent than a sigh.

Lizards scurry the fat cemetery walls.
The flesh-robbing fury of gluttonous
autumnal wasps drones, and glows.

Men sitting on the banks of ditches
watch the deep fires of death,
the smell of dense mold is already afloat.

Flames dart over the road fluttering half-light half-blood!
Burning brown leaves
buck weakly in the wind.

Clusters fall, vine shoals withering,
the stalks of yellow flowers rattle
as the seeds spin off.

The meadow swims in twilit mist.
Savage clatter of distant wagons
shaking off the last leaves.

The countryside fallen asleep,
death glides in on white, beautiful wings,
the sky nurses the garden.
And in your hair: look! A golden autumn leaf—
a branch wept above you.

O dearest, flare about autumn, above death,
and lift me too! Have the wisdom to love
now, the wisdom to kiss, to hunger for sleep.

Love joyfully, don't leave me—
plunge with me into the blackened sky of sleep.
Let us sleep. Outside: the thrush is already dozing,
walnuts drop onto leaf-mold now
without a tap—and reason deteriorates.

10 October 1941

The Angel of Dread

Today, the angel of dread, invisible,
and silent in me, does not shriek.
But, at a squeak, you are startled—
at merely the snap of a grasshopper
you turn, but who was it?
It was him. Only, today he is cautious—but poised!
Protect me because you love me. Love me heroically.
When you are with me, he sulks; he is fierce
when you leave me alone. He rises from the pit of the soul
and, screaming, accuses me.
Madness. Working into me like poison,
rarely letting up. Living inside,
also outside. When a moonlit night is white,
in whizzing sandals he dashes the meadow,
rummaging about in my mother's grave.
"Was it worth it?" he keeps asking her,
rousing her, whispering, inciting her, strangling:
"You gave birth to him and it killed you!"
Occasionally, he looks at me,
tearing off the calendar pages that were awaiting their turn.
How far and where to
now depend upon him forever. His word,
a stone into water,
dropped into my heart last night,
gyrating, swinging, revolving.
I was just about to go to bed,
you were already asleep. I stood still,
naked, when he arrived
and began to quietly argue with me here.
A peculiar scent was afloat, a chilling
breath at my ear. "Keep on undressing,"
he urged, "not even skin should defend you—
you are, after all, raw flesh and bare nerve.

Flay yourself, for he is a fool
who brags about his skin, his prison.
Skin is only an *appearance* about you.
Come on! Take this knife—
it won't hurt, will only take a minute, one wince!"

On the table, in a blaze, the knife awakened.

4 August 1943

Seventh Eclogue

Do you see? Evening falls, fringed with barbed-wire,
the hacked-out oak fence and barracks waver, sucked up by dusk.
The framework of our captivity is undone by a hesitant gaze
and the mind alone—the mind alone—knows the tautness of the wire.
Do you see, dearest, imagination here can free itself only this way.
By dreaming, that beautiful liberator, our broken bodies are unleashed,
in that moment the prison camp starts home!
In rags, heads shaved, snoring, the prisoners fly
from Serbia's blind heights to the hiding homelands.
The hiding homelands? O is our home still there?
Maybe no bomb touched it? Might it be, as when we were drafted?
The one groaning on my right, the one sprawling on my left,
    will they return home?
Tell me, is there still a homeland where this hexameter will be understood?

Without accent marks, feeling out line after line,
here, in the dusk, I write this poem just as I live,
blindly, a caterpillar inching my way on the paper.
Flashlight, book, everything taken away by the Lagar guards,
and there's no mail—only fog settles on our barracks.
Among false rumors and worms, here in the mountains live
Frenchmen, Poles, loud Italians, Serbian separatists, and brooding Jews,
a chopped up, fevered body, still living one life,
waiting for good news, woman's beautiful word, free human fate,
waiting for the end that drops into dense twilight, for the miracle.

I am lying on a plank, a captive animal among worms,
the fleas' assault starts up again, but the army of flies are at rest.
It is night, one day shorter again, you see,
and, one day shorter, life. The camp is sleeping. The landscape
lit by the moon. In its light, the wire is again taut.
One can see through the window, cast on the wall,
shadows of armed guards passing among the night sounds.

The camp is sleeping, do you see, dearest, dreams are rustling,
a startled man snorts, tosses about in his tight space,
already back to sleep, his face radiates. Only I sit up awake,
I feel a half-smoked cigarette in my mouth instead of the taste of your kiss,
and sleep, the comforter, does not come,
for I cannot die nor live without you anymore.

Lagar Heidenau, in the mountains
above Zagubica, July 1944.

Root

Through the root power flashes unseen,
the root drinks rain, feeds on earth
and its dream is falling white snow.

Earth-embedded it strives to burst earth,
it crawls cunningly, the root does,
its arm like uncoiling rope.

On the root's arm, a worm sleeps,
on the root's foot, a worm sits.
The world becomes wormy, wormsick.

But below, the root lives on and on,
it is not concerned with the world,
only with a foliage-lush branch.

That branch it feeds and adores,
sending up delicious flavors,
sweet, heavenly flavors...

I too am a root now,
I'm living among worms,
down there this poem is being formed.

I was a flower. I became a root.
Leaden, black soil covers me,
my fate has been fixed.
A saw shrieks above my head.

Lager Heidenau, in the mountains
above Zagubica, August 8, 1944.

Serbian Postcard 1

From Bulgaria, the roll of thick, wild cannon blasts
beat against the ridge, resonate, fade...
humans beasts wagons thoughts amass,
the road rears whinnying, maned sky bolts.
In this mobile chaos you are constant in me,
in the pit of my consciousness you shine, motionless
forever, mute, like the angel, while admiring destruction,
or an insect, burying itself in the cavity of a tree's decay.

30 August 1944
in the mountains

Forced March

He is a fool who, collapsed on the ground, gets up and walks on,
like a wandering pain, he moves ankle and knee,
yet starts out again, like one lifted by wings.
In vain, the ditch invites him, he doesn't dare to stay,
and if you ask him: why not? maybe he will still answer
he's expected by his wife, and by a wiser, more beautiful death.
But, this simple soul is a fool, for, over the homes,
a long time, scorched wind has been twisting,
the house wall has stretched out, the plum tree snapped,
the homeland night is woolly with fear...
O if only I could believe: not only in my heart do I bear all
that is worthwhile, and: there is a home to return to...
If it were still there as before, on the ancient cool veranda
the bees of peace would drone, while plum jam chills,
an end-of-summer quiet would sunbathe the drowsy garden,
among the foliage, fruit would sway naked,
Fanni would wait blondely before the russet hedge
and slow morning would write a shadow slowly...
surely it still can perhaps be! The moon tonight so immensely full!
Don't go on without me, my friends, shout at me!

And I push on...

Bor, September 15, 1944

Ferenc Juhász:
The Biography
of a Woman

She bore three sons. Has two sons. Was twenty-five
when she buried the third. Then, the children were given
chocolate milk. For breakfast! Chocolate milk and crescent rolls.
   Sunday. The man
did not drink wine. He drank onion tea from a white porcelain
   mug.
A mug of red onion water. This was the onion tea.
The red onion a smelly ball in the onion juice.
The man ate the onion too. The Globe that death ate.
He was operated upon two years ago. They cut out one lung.
Onions were requested, eggs, lard. Then the man drank
a cup of coffee, into the coffee he had put a soupspoon of lard,
into the coffee he had broken an egg. He mixed it all with the spoon,
   drank it.
But, he did not drink wine. The family was sitting around the
   kitchen table.
Jánoska was ten months old. Brain fever. Death.
Jánoska in a tiny blue coffin. In a tiny blue coffin on a table in
   the room.
Jánoska a wax lily. Jánoska a wax rose.
Jánoska a wax bear. A blond wax bear. Jánoska a yellow wax
   lizard.
A scaly newborn lizard. Jánoska a white-crested newt. Jánoska a
   dwarf-
Christmas-tree. Jánoska frozen angel hair. Jánoska a praying
   tadpole.
His wax fingers clasped in prayer. Tiny wax hands like a rainy slate tent.
His wax smile, black murky night. On his wax eyelids
the dew of holy water, like diamond dust on the tail of our Galaxy.
On Jánoska's ice heart nose tip a red goblin sits. And
   the patent-leather booted
goblin has seven heads, on seven scaly green towers, seven
   heads.

On seven necks, seven heads. On each head the face of an
   angel.
On each angel face a green gold beard. And there are fourteen
   eyeballs in the seven angel faces.
Like spinning tops, the goblin angel dragon heads turn.
Their eyes: Judgment, Grief, Fever, Slobbering, Crying,
   Coughing,
Mercilessness, Vomiting, Consciousness, Diarrhea, Heavy-
   breathing,
Guilty conscience, Accusation, Death. Jánoska a milky ear of
   corn with a blond
silky beard. And mournful butterfly wings with fiery rings
pinned with a silver safety-pin to the back of the dragon angel
   goblin.
Under the fiery ringed butterfly wings, red dragonfly wings:
pinned there with a silver safety-pin. The window in the room
   open.
Through the window in the door, people looking. Children on
   tiptoes.
Adults wiping their noses. On the white crocheted window
   curtain,
the white crocheted wings of praying angels crocheted from
   squares of yarn
flapping numbly. The bell tolls. The death bell.
In the farmyard, those who came for the funeral are gathering.
Already there: the little blue Saint-John carrying Blue Saint
   Michael's Horse.
And the horses drawing the Horse are girls clad in white,
with white myrtle wreaths, white rose wreaths, on their heads.
Their hair let down to their shoulders, to their waists. Their
   plaits unbraided. And let down.
She was a servant girl, a day-laborer girl, a brick-layer girl,
she worked at the sack-sewing factory and she also worked in a
   chocolate factory. She cooked,
she did the laundry, washed dishes, cleaned the house, a child-
   servant. Ten years old, with

a Jewish family. She waxed floors. Escorted the older girls to
     school.
Carried their suitcases, their net bags. "Those girls always ran
     away,
they also ate dates." When the family was not at home, she
     would sit at
the piano, striking at the keys with her red child hands.
Proletarian girl Chopin, proletarian girl Franz Liszt, proletarian
     girl Arthur
Rubenstein. Dishwater, lye, soapy water, corridor-scrubbing
     water,
frost: these tiled red gloves on her hands. Red animal gloves for
     her hands.
She carried mortar in a cement-skinned bucket up to the
     scaffoldings,
carried bricks on fodder racks, pushed brick-loaded carts.
"In the sack-sewing factory, I used to wrestle with the other
     girls. And my fingers were like
a swollen pin-cushion, the tips of my fingers like little violet
     melons.
Masses of pin-prick points. Eddies of pin-wound points."
She traveled to Budapest by train at 5 AM. To the station.
She was blind for five years as a child. If no one led her,
she totter-walked. Like snail tentacles pushing out from eye-
     mushrooms,
with a spirally bubbling, her hands, arms, staggered in the air,
smacking well wheels, walls, fence rails, trees, hens, flowers,
and terrified by what they smacked drew back under her tender
     armpits.
The others did not take her to a doctor. Nor did she know what
     the disease was. She was blind.
A blind little servant with her rich relatives. "You can also see
     my blindness in this faded
photo. That's me there in the middle." In the faded photo her
     Schwabian relatives:

Uncle János, Aunt Náni. On Uncle János: brown boots, braided
    brown trousers,
a short brown coat with skeletal braiding. A yellow shirt with
    butterfly-wing
collar. His head bare. Hands on his knees. Eyes light-givingly
    dead. On Aunt
Náni: brown-buttoned shoes, a brown skirt reaching to the
    ground. A brown bodice with
mother-of-pearl rose buttons. Tight short coat. Her head bare.
Her hands on her dyed-blue Schwabian apron, crease-squared
    from ironing and folding.
The apron like Simon Hantai's creased, folded, drawn out blue,
    violet, brown and
green canvases! Tile-blue Virgin Mary aprons!
The Virgin Mother's tile-blue Cosmos-apron! The mama-
    yearnings!
The mama-sobs! The mama-sadnesses! The mama-prayers!
Christmas. Easter. Pentecost. The Lord's Day. The Blessing of the
    Wheat.
Church Fair. The Assumption. Weddings. Christenings. Funerals.
    The eyes of
Aunt Náni: light-givingly dead! Between, the blind servant.
The thirteen year old. Her apron a brown child-Universe.
In her right hand a yellow daisy. Her left hand on Uncle János'
    shoulder.
Around her neck a white four-strand necklace. Her braided
    brown hair in a basket-wreath.
And her eyes: blind graveyards! Her eyes: blind graveyards! Her eyes:
blind jelly roses! Her eyes: snot blind glass colts. Dead glass
    calves.
Her eyes: frozen cow mouths. Her eyes: frosty tiny Virgin
    Mother heads.
Her eyes: blinded visions. Her eyes: the locked diamond-gate of
    heaven.
Her eyes: the two shut gate-wings of the underworld!

"My mother healed me. She rubbed my eyes with powdered
     sugar.
She rubbed my eyes with powdered sugar in the morning, at
     noon, and in the evening, with powdered sugar.
And she put cobwebs on them. Sparrow shit. And pigeon
     droppings. She put tea-soaked wet
packs on them. Picked herbs, medicinal grass, medicinal
     flowers, at the pond's edge.
I don't know their names. She made tea out of them, and with
     the tea kept washing
my blind eyes. She washed them, kept on washing them with
     hard fingers. My eyes,
like the newborn. Like the newborn when they break out
     bloodily from a woman.
First their hair, then their faces, then their heads almost
     exploding
the lower part of her body, according to the faith like Jesus burst
out of damnation, when one's legs are like the arms of the cross
and one rips apart from anus to navel! Mama used to wash my
     eyes
like mother's blood from the newborn, like embryo grease,
like embryo saliva dirt from the newborn's mouth, like embryo
     tar from their nostrils.
She hung a sachet of medicinal herbs on a string around
     my neck.
I used to walk with the scented sachet like a gold chain around
     my neck.
My friend, Aunt Szabó led me. And we played with knives,
     running around
each other with long kitchen knives. With knives.
My mother healed my blind eyes!" She took in washing and
     ironing for money.
Forty kilograms of laundry each week. On Tuesday she washed,
     on Wednesday
dried the laundry, on Thursday she ironed. The little tanner's
     sumac was brooding

over its green prehistory near the draw well. And it shed blood
in the autumn,
like the face of the crucified Christ, like his temples, his heart
wound, his hands, legs, dangling
from the nails. In the yard, on clotheslines suspended between
trees, white
towels and white cotton coats used to dry. They also used to dry
in the earthen
breath of the attic. In winter, like glass flames—in summer,
steaming
pages of an epic. The man used to bring the bundle of clothing.
Drunk, sober, her husband brought it. Brought it in brown
wrapping paper,
in a forty kilogram paper bag tied into a big square with knotted
string.
He brought it sober, and he brought it drunk. On Monday he
brought it home,
on Friday, he took it back. On Friday he took it back, on
Monday he brought it home.
He brought it from Budapest. Took it back to Budapest.
Her husband loved wine and soda. He drank this from a big
glass.
Beer only at the summer fair when the band was playing.
He would sit there,
a grey rabbit-pelt hat tilted back on his head, his tie loosened
in a white shirt, his jacket on a chair. His shirt sleeves rolled up
to his elbows,
up to the red elastic bands. He got off the train, the bundle on
his slanting shoulder.
First the train station pub. There: cards. Then on the way home,
another pub. A game of "rex," wine and soda. At the third pub,
wine and soda.
Billiards. He chalked the cold black nose of the cue and
guffawed
when he hit the white bone ball stylishly. The dog always knew
where he was.

It barked one way when he got off the train with the brown
    bundle
and when he started home staggering, barked another way.
The man used to crawl on all fours in the mud. To chortle in the
    rain.
He grunted, cried, crawled smilingly. His forehead, his tongue,
    his mouth,
the inside of his mouth, all were muddy, his shirt and pants,
    muddy. His genitals muddy. Between
his freckled fingers, webs of mud. His eyeballs also muddy.
But he always brought the bundle. He always took the bundle.
And he could hardly believe she was paid merely four pengos!
The children trembled. The woman: "You tell your father!"
And she threw the alarm clock at him. Her scissors.
Threw the lamp at him, her husband jumping aside, chortling.
    Like a blazing angel,
like a crazed star. The lamp flew into the front yard. It smashed
    through the window,
flaming, glass splintered and the front yard was ablaze.
The tanner's sumac ablaze, the jasmine bush, and the roses
    flamed, the lilies blazed.
"Will I go blind? I have already received my blind person's
    pension.
I appealed for it, it is due me, it is nothing to be ashamed of, for
    a poor woman.
But I do not want a blind person's cane, although they want to
    give me one.
I don't want a white cane or an iron cane, I don't want to grope
    along with a cane,
to grope along in the fog. Must I tap left, right, with a crooked
    white iron cane?"
And she gazes into the crystal silence, she gazes with a crystal
    smile.
Not to where they are, nor where they speak from. Gazes with a
    savior face,

gazes as if He were there! She gazes with a mist-lit face, gazes
    with her forehead.
"One of my ears is punctured. A blind and deaf old woman. I
    have tunnel vision.
The doctor said: 'it doesn't matter, auntie, at least you do not
    see,
at least you do not see the evil!'" And she hoes, digs in the
    garden,
prunes vines, ties up rose vines, goes to the store,
pickles cucumbers and cans peaches. After the war,
during the removal, she was on the "list" too. Had no idea why,
but she was on the "list." She sat there on her kitchen stool,
    having just collected
the eggs, boring her index finger into the hens' bottoms to feel
    with the tip of her finger
the egg in the hen's body. Or to pull out the fluffy, bloody
lime sphere from the hen's ass, to excite the hen to lay.
She was sitting on the kitchen stool, her husband was poking
    around in the garden.
In the middle of the kitchen: the big clothes basket with a
    bunched-up quilt,
pots, mugs, spoons, jam bottles, sausages, all kinds of things.
The basket covered with a gold floral-patterned scarlet
    bedspread,
tied down all around, like the soaked cellophane of the
    preserves glass,
with a rubber string, or with a regular string if there was nothing
    else.
And the neighbor woman came: "I will take the ducks. They will
    only die here."
Later, between two doors, with her little girl between her knees,
    a mere five years old,
the neighbor woman stood whimpering. Out in the street,
    people screamed:
"Her son is a Communist! Hang this one too! Together with her
    sniveling brat!

108

At another time, she was guarding a sick person.

Guarding a schizophrenic. The shield of depression. The snail
    shell of mania.

The one in a checkered flannel shirt, with yellow corduroy
    pants, did not eat,

did not drink, just sat. Did not drink, did not eat, just stood.

He was watching the sunset, the brain-evening, for two years.
    The white mind-midnight.

He slept, read, got up. Slept, read, gazed. Was gazing at winter,
    at autumn.

Was gazing at summer, at spring. And he began to scream, he
    ran in September.

In freckled autumn, running, he screamed, sobbing.

He was smashing a whole basket of eggs to the ground. He
    smashed the eggs

one by one on the stone kitchen floor! He first took one into his
    hand,

turned it, examining it, balancing the lime bubble on his
    fingertips,

then smashed it to the stone, as if he had hugely hockered.

He was smashing them, they really splattered, he was smashing
    them, how they squirted!

Gazing with windhover eyes, gazing with hawk eyes, with snake
    eyes,

gazing with a knife glance and a spatter, and the kitchen floor

suddenly a yellow glaze, snot honey egg white, suddenly lime
    shell half-bubbles, suddenly

a lime shell potsherd dunghill. As if a crazed monster had
    vomited, as if madness

spewed bile on the Universe. The Madness Gall-Bladder was
    pouring out its stinking fluid.

And his hand was bilely, the wall also spattered with bile. In the
    yard:

the woman running around. The other one after her. After her
    with a big knife.

With a pig-killing bayonet! "You whore, whore, whore, you
    whore!" he yelled,
and she: "he'll jump into the well!" The bayonet belongs to his
    father, who brought it back
from Isonzo. Where he was shot in the belly. Later he was
    buried at home.
The hens were also flapping about, they were racing around
    squawking, the dog wailed on its chain,
the rooster crowed, crowed blackly. Blackly for the third time.
And the pig grunted like a drunken Buddha, and the goose flew
through autumn like the Revelations of Saint John. And the
    neighbors were watching,
crowding the fence, thronging the pickets, watching and
    shrieking with laughter.
The woman: an old woman. But a never-old-woman. She has
    five grandchildren.
Two great-grandchildren. Her hands move easily. Her feet are
    quick too.
And in her memory, Eden is not Hell! She does not regularly
    visit the graveyard.
She doesn't love it or hate it. She goes there on All Saint's Day,
    or on All Soul's.
Takes an armful of flowers, a bouquet for each family grave.
When she gets back home, she washes her hands "because after
    the graveyard,
one washes one's hands. This is the proper thing to do.
For the graveyard is dirty, the graveyard is dead.
Also, after washing the dead, when we have washed the naked
    dead,
their faces, breasts, chests, bellies, the maleness, the femaleness,
    and the thighs,
legs and feet, when we have wiped everything, then we also
    have to wash our hands."
She is reading something right now. Maybe a book of poems.
    For she too wrote poems!

"As if I heard it now too: O how proud this girl is!" She reads,
  looks at
the quiet. As if she were looking at the world through the shaft
  of a straw.
At the end of the emptiness-stuffing in the yellow straw shaft,
in the air-lens of the round straw husk, in the air-disc,
hardly anything can be seen. Half-orchards, half-photos, half of
  a long-haired doll
split as if by a sickle, old, hair-torn, one-eyed.
What the emptiness-plate of the round straw husk shows,
  enclosed in its husk-rim encasement.
One doll nostril. The cotton in the gash between the petals of
  the celluloid face rose.
And everything is as tiny in the straw ring, in the thin shaft of
  the straw,
as in the Land of Lilliput. She sees it the way we make light
  with a torch at night:
the yellow rod of light, the light dust-gold rod painting a little
  gold
circle on the dark. In the gold rod, a dewy beetle, a daisy,
a dew dust-winged velvet butterfly, a lemon butterfly, a cabbage
  butterfly.
As the torch light stabs a point of fire into the dark, a gold pin
  into the night.
She sees as an ophthalmologist does when with a little penlight
he illuminates the eyeball body through the pupil, he sees
the purple blot, the veined disc of the retina, the ribbon-feelered
  soft
sun disc veined with light. Scarlet map in the dark. Scarlet
  flower island,
scarlet continent with rivers, the earth from a space ship.
"And tell me, that Allende, was he on the side of the poor?" she
  asked,
brooding. "Of *course*, I saw him once on TV." Maybe she is
  looking at herself.

Her husband died in her arms, vomited blood, "mama mama,"
    he cried.
There was blood on his chest, blood on the woman's hands. He
    died in her arms.
After the funeral, they scrubbed the floor until dawn, she and
    her sister-in-law.
Her mother died in her arms. But she recedes colorfully, like a
    beautiful dream.
She lived with her younger son, then with her elder son, now
    with her grown granddaughter.
What does this woman read? This not not-old old woman?
"Like a few thin spikes driven into the soil,
Spires appeared on the horizon at dawn.
But they were so small, that the shepherd boy
Glimpsed them as if peering through a straw!"
Indeed, this is János Arany. Indeed, this is his *The Village Fool!*

1986

Note:

The words "removal" and "list" refer either to the forced removal to Germany of
ethnic German peasants after 1945, because of their assumed complicity with
Nazism, or the forced removal in the early 1950s, the Stalinist period, of class
aliens to labor camps. Among these, so-called "kulák" families were also removed
on extremely unfounded grounds (if there were any grounds for the whole
process at all). "List" is the so-called "Kulák list" which every village council kept
on record for the regular retaliations, confiscations, and extra taxes that the more
well-off farmers were subjected to. The villagers screaming "Her son is a
Communist" in the poem is a response to October 1956 when in some cases
people sought revenge on Communist neighbors for Stalinist practices.

[GK]

Sandor Csoori:
The Visitor's Memories

I left a piece of my head in that smoky-smelling house, there, right there on the milk-burnt plain of the oven-top, with the bread crust tossed to the dog. I arrived, uninvited early in the morning. At first, the waking children merely stared at me from behind the fortifications of their bunched-up quilts: who might I be? what might I want? in what shop did I steal my camomile-yellow shoes? But when I discovered, one by one, their bud-like noses and geranium ears, and before their very eyes did a hairy bear-fist waddle, "grr-grr-grr, my skin is bitten by fleas, the fleas are biting my knees," I saw the little bishops of laughter consecrated by merriment. Their tiny bread-like teeth exploded through the room like popcorn. From the blackened table to the stool, from the stool to earthen floor, down to the sandals tossed under the beds. More! More! Don't take the bear away once you have brought him here (their timid mouths would have said had they expressed themselves).

Out of one eye their mother watched the theater tumbling out of nowhere. Instead of cat-flaying excitement, or bear-flaying blood adventure, she noticed marching clouds reined in by the serenity in the children's dilated eyes. She continued sitting on her hatchet-hewed milking-stool, drinking her eternal cup of tea. I knew that the sun sets in her liver, that the years support her ramshackle heart with a wooden beam. I also knew that with her blackening dried-plum face, I would appear beneath frosty chandeliers at drink-nursing diplomatic feasts where, wrapped in lettuce, her prematurely-harvested breasts would also be served.

I will arrive at such dinners perhaps by plane, perhaps with iron-plated wings attached to my shoulders, perhaps on the back of a leaf drifting in through an open window, I, the spy for the poor, who is blessed with destroyer eyes and who sees everything. My ironed shirt will be the skin of those who have been sophisticatedly flayed, my Golgothically ticking clock their pounding temples, after those of my father, my mother, and this sister as well, sitting before me, the orphan of a familiar but vanishing story, harboring no impassioned revenge, in tea steam breathing through her children's mouths and surviving through her children's flesh the tribute exacted from her womb.

1977

Enikö Bollobás:
A Personal Report on the
Present Situation of the
Hungarian Writer, Géza Szöcs

I would like to draw your attention to the severe situation of a talented Hungarian writer in Rumania, Géza Szöcs, aged 32, who is suffering from the raging persecution of the Rumanian authorities.

This is a man who did nothing more than write. He wrote memoranda, petitions and proposals, and submitted them to the Madrid Conference, the Ottawa Human Rights Experts' Meeting and to the Central Committee of the Rumanian Communist Party. He addressed the Rumanian Communist Party several times because he did not consider his proposals either subversive or illegal. The rights he demanded had all been guaranteed under the Rumanian constitution. Szöcs engaged in the legitimate exercise of the right to freedom of expression provided under the Helsinki Final Act, to which Rumania is a signatory. The object of his petitions was not only legitimate, but far from radical. All the items he requested were ones that had already existed after the introduction of Communism in Rumania, during the postwar regime of Prime Minister Petru Groza. The requested reforms would in no way threaten or inhibit the existing political, economic or social order in Rumania.

But Rumania is a country where only one nation, one culture, one church is tolerated: the Rumanian. Where Hungarian and German minorities are not permitted to maintain cultural institutions or any organizations which could defend their rights, either as individuals or as minorities.

There are no Hungarian schools in Rumania, whereas such schools had existed previously for centuries. There are only Hungarian classes, which can only be formed under the strictest of regulations, where the language of instruction in the sciences, history and geography is Rumanian.

There is no Hungarian university in Rumania. A bilingual institution, created in 1958 when the 150-year-old Hungarian university of Kolozsvár was closed down, has suffered a radical decrease in Hungarian-language instruction in the humanities, and in subjects embodying the particular culture of national minorities. In 1985, a total of only 5 students were admitted to study Hungarian literature and to become teachers of

Hungarian. This is the number allotted to 2.5 million Hungarians, the largest national minority in Europe. The only drama school to train Hungarian actors has also become bilingual.

All cultural relations between Rumania and Hungary, but especially between the Hungarian minority and Hungary, have been eliminated. There are no international cultural events in Rumania, nothing that would promote European cultural exchange.

Existing Hungarian and German television and radio broadcasts in Rumania were completely eliminated early this year. Public statues of Hungarian and German historical figures have all been demolished, and those that have been erected in their place are ones that portray figures whose sole function is to further the animosity between Rumanians and the minorities.

Rumania is a Communist country where only one church is tolerated: the Rumanian Orthodox Church. Among the many institutions of this national church we can find the flourishing monasteries of Moldavia. But no other denominations have been allowed to maintain their own monasteries. Rumania is a country where priests are beaten to death and Bibles are recycled into toilet paper.

Rumania is a country where censorship exists already in the dreams and thoughts of the writer: a pre-natal censorship, the abortion of thought before it can even come to life. And where this pre-natal censorship fails, and a thought is born, its bearer suffers the cruelest retaliation.

The persecution of Szöcs is not only persistent, but expert, ingenious, and determined. Up until October 15, he spent 8 to 10 hours a day in the interrogation room. He cannot use his typewriter, because as soon as he tries to, the police break in. All his manuscripts, his notes and personal letters are confiscated. His telephone is bugged, he does not receive any mail whatsoever. Whoever he talks to in the street must report the conversation to the police. He is denied his passport, and letters if invitation sent by French, German or Hungarian universities never arrive. He cannot publish his works or pursue his career. In the streets he is followed, day and night, and his apartment is bugged. He lives in a social vacuum artificially created by the Rumanian authorities.

Allow me to quote a few passages from the letters he managed to send through dangerous channels. The final word should be his. These words reflect the horrific atmosphere in which a European writer must live in 1985:

"Don't ever be surprised if you hear someone quoting the exact words of our most intimate conversations— what we talked about in the car, in bed or out in the fields. I've heard such tapes; they've played them to me several times."

"I have seen photographs of us. For example, when we were stepping out of that old Lutheran church in X, remember? You look so beautiful in that picture, holding the ominous book they were after. Even the bookmark is clearly visible: 'Except the Lord build the house, they labor in vain to build it; except the Lord keep the city, the watchmen waketh but in vain.'"

"No dramatist can imagine such a situation: I am sitting in the interrogation room, under the spotlights, and because these bright lights are directed straight into my eyes, my tears keep falling— they are running down my face all the while, and in the meantime they read our letters to me. This crude voice coming from the darkness behind me, reading the lines dearest to me... I would once like to write all this down as dramatically as it really happened, but I don't think I'll be able to. At least, not for a long time."

"I am exhausted and need all my strength to finish this letter; they could break in at any moment. The candle is running out (and, you know, especially around all Saints' Day, you cannot buy candles in town), my fingers are trembling, and I cannot see —spending each day under bright lights and fists, each night in candlelight. And this is my last candle."

1985

Géza Szöcs:
Commentary on
an Old Review

(Billboard-poetry: ambiguous, harsh, journalistic):
Arpád Visky gravediggers, have you called a conference,

                              a production seminar,
have you called a brief meeting, a meeting? what was it like,

                              was it successful?
who's the head gravedigger?

                    Hey sutler wenches, what's going on?
Have you heard that Arpi died?

                    friends everywhere tomorrow!
Or will there be any?! who knows!
is anyone mourning? who are the mourners?
gravediggers! are we on schedule?
is anyone still unburied?

                    Goddamn it, shovelers!
you must increase production!

*

September 6, 1980, Saturday night, 7:30.[1] *As I entered the foyer of the Hungarian Theater, there between two pillars, in a glass cage with wooden bars, with absolute authenticity, was Visky Arpád. He was moving about, pacing back and forth, pathetically, lit up by a spotlight like an insect, scratching at the glass with such silent helplessness that the audience clustering about him in a big circle could not really enjoy what they were seeing. ALL THIS IS LIKE AN ACCI-DENT ON THE STREET, someone next to me said, and it really was like an accident. Yes, for stage events take us by surprise in a different way than real events, and in this case the spectacle was especially powerful because it allowed one to forget that he was in a theater. Yes: Tompa, the Director, and Visky, managed—and this is the utmost—to communicate to the audience in such a way that they forgot that what they were seeing was theater.*

*

Do not think that we forgot you.[2]
Once, we nearly opened our mouths to speak out—
but, well, there were so many excused absences.

Gum mushrooms,
especially mushrooms on the gums,
and mouth bloat,
diptheria
and uvulitis, and heart obesity:

so you see, with such sicknesses, it is very difficult.
But tell us, Arpád Visky,
what play did you put on for your jailers?[3]
Did they get your political skits?
what is the Danube-delta like in winter?
   (Billboard-poetry, indeed!) just how happy
would you say a delta labor camp is?
What did you put on for the prisoners, your fellow prisoners

and for the mice laborers and for the birds in the reeds?
ARPAD VISKY, TO WHOM DO YOU PLAY IN THE GRAVE?
who is your audience: deadolescents? or the earth spirit, the geo-demon?
is it your voice I now hear? "I am playing Tatrangi"

are you playing[4] Tatrangi at the moment he touches down?
the way your favorite hero, David Tatrangi, when he lands,
has his hand on the direction stick,
standing in his flying machine with flapping wings,
the way he lands Home
      in Jókai's Utopia[5].
most certainly this is your role in the earth.

                                   *

Good news!
the Hungarians have won the world cup in tiddly-winks.
His Holiness the Pope prayed for us.

Light is thrown upon mysterious forces all the time. A noose hangs
   between the laws.

Possibly, the missing 80% of the universe has been recovered.
The Fifth Reciprocal Effect has been discovered:
but all this is of no use to you, Arpád Visky.
And I feel this poem isn't good enough.

Let's do it rabbit eye fashion,
                boiled lobster fashion,
si nu mai scrium poezii bune,
and we do not yet good poetry write,
and no force or Reciprocal Effect has untied
the noose around your neck

staring each other out in a blood-smeared obituary:
the suffering
                and the reckoning.

*

Arpád Visky is one of our most talented actors, but this time, in the role of Woyzeck, this man whose personality has been smacked and kicked out of him, this miserable person who has been driven mad, perhaps because he was in bad form? was he oppressed by some dark presentiment in connection with his role? anyway: that night except for a few outstanding moments, he was unable to perform brilliantly, the way he usually does.

Still, as I wrote in my review six years ago:

From now on, whenever I pass through the foyer of the theater, I will always think of Visky as a monument of defenselessness and helplessness, and he will be more vividly present for me than those stone statues of theatrical notables exhibited there that we seldom notice.

The Fifth Force, the Black Reciprocal Effect
lurks behind gravity,
with two hands, with a yellow bandanna, it helps fruit to drop,
it leans out of the windows of the free fall,
adjusts the pillow under Visky's head.

> Rope, freedom and handicraft
> and acting and law all blend.
> A nigger is sleeping in the cotton-field
> and he who passes by, bows his head.

Notes

1.In the late 1970s/early 1980s, I worked as a non-party-member independent journalist for one of the "ruling" party's newspapers, The Truth, published in Kolozsvár, Rumania. The *italicized* parts of this text are word-for-word quotations from the review of a play in the September 9, 1980 edition of The Truth, which I wrote about the Woyzeck performance by the Sepsiszentgyörgy Company in Kolozsvár, directed by Tompa.

2. (From a letter written to Arpád Visky, November 1984): Last August I wrote an article on the plays Tompa has directed, at the request of the Het Weekly, and in it, when writing about Woyzeck, I remembered you in print. The Assistant Editorial Director phoned me immediately: they would publish my article, BUT OBVIOUSLY WITHOUT ANY REFERENCE TO VISKY— and, he added: I PRESUME YOU WERE JOKING. This was already six months after your arrest. Since I was not joking, I could not agree to the publication of the article. A few days later, I heard that this Assistant Editorial Director remembered our conversation in these words: had they agreed to publish the article as I wrote it, the following day the three main editors would have been dismissed. "Perhaps it is all the same to Szöcs, but certainly not to us," this otherwise fine and good-intentioned Assistant Editorial Director added, who, strange as it may seem, along with his boss, was fired a few weeks later in spite of all this watchfulness and caution. Well, in that case, they might as well have published the article mentioning you, I might add now— if

one is going to get fired regardless, it is all the same, no? Of course, if this article does get published, everyone will be certain that it has something to do with the firing of the editors, and I will be the scapegoat! "That man only brings trouble."

Something else: through Andris Visky, I contacted some Transylvanian actors now living in Hungary, with a request that they select some poems for a public reading, or set up some other kind of performance, and turn the proceeds over to you, not mainly for the money, but as a public show of solidarity.

Months later, the answer came and it was this: why us?

3. (Excerpts from some broodings)
For example, the poet can write for his desk drawer, as well as the composer, and even the painter who has been locked out of society can be duly appreciated by future generations. But what hope is there for an actor, locked up in a prison cell, exiled from his stage?

4. (From a letter to Visky, November 1984): Thus I don't have time right now to turn Mór Jókai's novel into a play, but I promise to do so in a few months. The question is, of course: where could it be performed? And could you be invited to play the leading role? As I see it, no theater here would touch it.

5. Re. this Utopia: according to Jókai's prophecy, as he put it in The Novel of the Future, in the 1960s there will be formed a utopian state in the Danube-delta under the leadership of David Tatrangi, which will be a republic of plenty, liberty, and equality. "He who travels toward the Black Sea along the river, when leaving Tulcsa, traveling on the Szulina fork on his own electric boat, will see on both banks permanent garden cities... he will see an infinite line of mansions... and magnificent hotels along the promenades... There is no prison in this Utopia... In this Utopia no one's life or freedom are endangered."

Epilogue

Arpád Visky was a man dissatisfied with himself. In the autumn of 1982, this is how I expressed his self-critical, self-ironical stance:

> When I was a child (he muses for a long time)
> I was exchanged (by mistake). I was exchanged
> (he twists his palms outward) for a poor and pitiable
> gypsy kid, and I often (he becomes sad) think
> about this: that the poor, real Arpi Visky shivers
> in a gypsy tent in the rain and cold somewhere
> while all this time (he gets angry) this fucking
> gypsy kid (pounding his chest) lives like a king
> and (he tosses down a shot) drinks and—(hand wave
> of resignation)

1986

Editorial note: Arpád Visky, until his arrest in January, 1983 was the leading actor of a Hungarian theater company in Transylvania, Rumania. Imprisoned on false political charges (he had insulted members of the Rumanian Secret Police on duty in the cafeteria of the theater), he spent the next two years in Danube-delta labor camps. After his release in the fall of 1984, he was banned from performing on any stage in Rumania and was forced to work as an unskilled laborer. On January 5, 1986, the Rumanian authorities staged a suicide: Visky's body was found hung in a remote forest outside Sepsiszentgyörgy by a local policeman minutes after the onset of death. His wife was not allowed to view the body. Prior to his death, Visky had repeatedly been denied immigration to Hungary.

Clayton Eshleman:
A Note on Vladimir Holan
and his *Hamlet*

I first heard of Vladimir Holan the summer of 1976, when Jan Benda, one of my students at the Frenstat "Summer Seminar," repeatedly mentioned his name, saying things like, "you don't have anyone like him in American poetry," which of course aroused my interest. At the end of the seminar, with a few free days in Prague at my disposal, I decided to try to find Holan. He was seventy-one at the time, famous *and* unknown; his work had been officially ignored from 1948 to 1963, and during this period he became a total recluse. He began to be published again in 1963, and received some international attention in the mid-to-late 1960s. However, a pattern had been established during the years of his utter neglect, and he never re-entered social life. Benda knew where the house was—on the tiny Kampa island of the Vltava River in central Prague—and made me a little map.

It turned out that the Holans (Vladimir, his wife, and their mentally handicapped, mute daughter) had moved. Had I not literally bumped into a Czech actress in the gateway leading to the Kampa house (who then spent an hour with me knocking on doors and stopping passers-by until a man on a bicycle gave us the new Holan address) I would have never found him. I never did meet Holan himself. With Mrs. Englander that morning (who had just returned to Prague from Vienna after an absence of twenty years), and three years later with Benda and the poet Milan Exner, I stood outside the Holan doorway and via my interpreters spoke with Mrs. Holan. While the poet, bed-ridden at the time, was not unfriendly (he sent out presents both times—a special edition of *A Night with Hamlet*, and a tiny leather-bound collection of short poems), he also was not receiving visitors. He died in 1980, still for the most part unknown in America.

In the late 1970s, I discovered that a version of *Hamlet* existed in English, and that several books had been translated into French.[1] While the Jarmila and Ian Milner version made me realize that the poem was very special, their version also felt inadequate—it was not the poem that Benda had praised. I began to look around Los Angeles for someone with whom to co-translate, and one of the people I spoke with, Frantisek Deak at UCSD, passed on my interest to his friend, Frantisek Galan, then at University of

Texas-Austin, who contacted me and offered his services. I decided that if we worked together side by side, and that if we showed our drafts to a third bilingual person, we could possibly produce a version of Hamlet that would be accurate *and* commanding in English. Besides the Milner version, we also had Dominique Grandmont's French version, and Galan's excellent English, with a knowledge of colloquialisms that many native-speakers lack. While we were making a first draft of Hamlet, we had laid out the English and French versions in front of our notebook; by the time we had finished a third draft, Galan felt that it had achieved the oddness, eloquence, and brusqueness of Holan's Czech, so we put the other versions aside, and did not go back to them. We went over our fourth draft with Michael Heim, who kindly spent several days with us in Austin in 1984. Both Galan and Heim had left "final-final" decisions up to me.

In the case of Artaud and Césaire, biographical materials abound, and while the European years of Vallejo are still shamefully unattended, it is still possible to get a sense of his European itinerary and his "life and contacts" there (especially since several people who knew him quite well in Paris were still alive and contactable when Barcia and I were revising my earlier translation in the 1970s). In Holan's case, I have no information that is not presented in the introductions to the translations cited in the footnote. I hesitate to repeat the scanty and possibly erroneous information of others, especially since there is no information whatsoever that I know of for the years in which Holan was composing Hamlet (1949-1956, 1962). Suffice it to say that from a glance at a brief bibliograpy, it is clear that he produced a massive body of work (it looks as broad and as international as Pound's), including translations of Gongora, Baudelaire, Rilke, Lermontov, Apollinaire, Eluard, and Tzara. Such an output was in part made possible by the fact that he took an early retirement from his job in a Prague pensions office, and after 1940 apparently devoted all of his time to writing.

In his Introduction to Vladimir Holan: Selected Poems, Ian Milner quotes from an interview with Holan that took place in 1964, the year that Noc s Hamletem was published:

> The years of writing A Night with Hamlet were the cruellest of my life. In my desperate loneliness I was well "earthed" to receive, and survive, all the horrors of that time. But it would be mistaken to think of

the poem as merely an expression of those particular events, since I have always been concerned with man and the human drama in general, with man's condition and unhappy lot, which he endures at all times... The question that was on my mind was: who was Hamlet?... I'm sure of one thing: for many tragic nights he became my companion. He stepped through the wall and there he was. We talked to each other... The conversations went on *ad infinitum*, not always tolerant, not always friendly, but always passionate. Something of those talks I've caught, I trust, in *A Night with Hamlet*.

Several relevant points can be drawn out of Holan's remarks. In ways that are hard to exactly determine, from where I am, it seems that the world of Holan's enwalled isolation, in which he seeks a ghost for companion, has reverberations with the world of Shakespeare's HAMLET (in capitals, henceforth, to distinguish him from Holan's figure); that Holan, feeling himself being sucked into a vortex of erasure, as a man, as a citizen, as a soul, as a writer, throws out a grapnel and it catches in HAMLET'S shoulder, the HAMLET who was forced to come to terms with an inner world because his outer world was warped with death, betrayal, and a false seeming. Holan drags his precursor (in effect, through the wall) into his studio, and the two, in mutual introduction, can certainly say to each other, almost in the same tone and meter, "the world is a prison in which there are many confines, wards, and dungeons, Denmark [Prague] being one of the worst."

Thinking of Holan being "out in the cold" during the years of *Hamlet's* composition, and having a sense of just how cold that cold can get, I am reminded of a story of a freezing man who discovered the carcass of a large animal; by cutting it open and enwombing himself within it, he saved his life. While such an analogy may seem a bit far-fetched, I believe that in *Hamlet*, Holan is saving his mind, and that without HAMLET as a "habitation" (and a name), he might very well have withered as a poet during this seven-year period (which in its own way oddly rhymes with Artaud's nine-year incarceration, during which time he was "disaffiliated"). Holan, having been erased by the State, discovers a cleft between "to be" and "not to be" in which, even though he does not exist socially-speaking, he can fulfill his obligation to being. He must do so as HAMLET was charged by his ghost to do: to act in a rotten world without becoming rotten himself.

In the interview Holan remarks that his main question was: who was Hamlet? When we consider what he turned HAMLET into, we must also consider that Shakespeare himself was drawing on sources that went back to the Icelandic Amlothi, and passed through the gamut of the skald Snaebjorn and Snorri Sturlason, Saxo Grammaticus, Belleforest and (it is assumed) Thomas Kyd. That is, HAMLET is not the single creation of a single author, but—and I think Holan would agree—is an evolving image of the poet as he dodges across the land-mine-filled fields of history, in metamorphosis on one level, eternally constant on another. So when HAMLET breaks through Holan's wall in 1949 Prague, he has become a one-armed sexual maniac obsessed with virgins who has access to characters (Juliet) in other Shakespearean plays; a multilingual world traveler; a gracious and acculturated philosopher who, in spite of his pessimism, honors motherhood and childlike innocence; and a mythological depository who contains a successfully returned Orpheus and Eurydice. He thus appears to be Dionysian and Titanic, rooted in Orphism, and faithful to the entire evolving history (and prehistory?) of HAMLET.

Furthermore, Hamlet is a particular kind of poetic soul: he is a "Mozart-swigger," obsessed with "atonal harmony" (evoking the music of Bartok, and the dissonance which has become one of the earmarks of 20th century art across the board), and as an "inspired" one is played off against the Holan-speaker's restraint. Both speakers in the poem dialogically create Hamlet; they comprise his inner dialogue with himself. In spite of its bizarre juxtapositions, morbidity and violent atmosphere, the poem is infiltrated with a kind of sad common sense about the world all human beings have made for each other, and thus it feels very rounded-out, even ripe, in spite of the dessication at its core.

For over three hundred years, directors and actors have cut and rewritten the script of HAMLET to suit their own purposes, to square it, as it were, with the morality of their times. Surely the speaker in Hamlet has this matter in mind when he says, early in the poem, "the yielding ripeness of Shakespeare/invites license" and follows these lines, a few lines later, with the image of the plays as apartments into which one after another "arrogant director" has moved. At the same time, Holan seems to be proposing that under such circumstances, he too be allowed "license" to recreate the

Hamlet I have described. And while his Hamlet is in no sense a simple imitation of HAMLET, the way the dialogue moves—via wordplays, split-second soliloquies, flashes of intelligence destabilized in the very act of being uttered, and most of all the associative "slides" in response and counter-response—is imaginatively true to the Shakespeare HAMLET'S mind.

If Césaire's *Notebook of a Return to the Native Land* is a masterpiece of heroic arrival, in which one can watch the symbolic incarnation of the poetic "self," Holan's *Hamlet* is a masterpiece of poetic maturity, the kind of poem many poets dream of writing in their early 50s, when they still have the physical stamina to be passionately exploratory, and when they have lived a full life that offers them vistas and roundness, and the confidence to embrace an earned sense of the human condition.

In Klaus Wagenbach's *Kafka par lui-même*, there is an extraordinary photo of Prague, a bird's-eye view, probably shot at dawn, with fog billowing amidst the black Gothic spires, the horned helmet-like towers, and the Byzantine cupolas. It is accompanied by the following quote, presumably from Kafka: "Prague does not release us... this little mother has claws." There is an eerie timelessness captured in this photo, a Prague of visionary vistas, menacing, ghostly, a Prague that evokes Holan's own "via negativa," the poet turned into a ghost by the State, a ghost who creates ghosts for company, and in doing so leaves a trace more enduring and vital than the State's imposed "silence."

Note

1. *A Night with Hamlet* (Tr. by Jarmila and Ian Milner, Oasis Books, London, 1980); see also *Vladimir Holan*: Selected Poems, by the same translators, Penguin Modern European Poets, 1971. There is also a recent second "selected poems" of Holan in English: *Mirroring*, tr. by C.G. Hanzlicek and Dana Habova (Wesleyan, 1985). The three French editions of Holan's poetry that I have found are all translated by Dominique Grandmont. They are: *Douleur*, Pierre Jean Oswald, Honfleur/ Paris, 1967; *Une nuit avec Hamlet*, Gallimard, 1968; and *Histoires*, Gallimard, 1977.

Vladimir Holan:

A Night with Hamlet

FOR VLADIMIR JUSTL

PUBLISHED FOR THE 400TH ANNIVERSARY

OF SHAKESPEARE'S BIRTH, IN 1964

Menippus: I see only bones and fleshless skulls, and most of
    them look alike.
Hermes: That's the very thing that has astonished all the poets,
    those bones... And only you, it seems, are contemptuous of them.
Menippus: Well then, show me Helen, for I wouldn't recognize
    her.
Hermes: This skull, that's Helen...

—Lucian

When passing from nature to being
walls are not exactly benevolent,
walls pissed on by the talented, walls spat on
by eunuchs revolting against the spirit, walls no smaller,
even if they are still unborn,
yet walls rounding out the fruit...

The yielding ripeness of Shakespeare
invites license. Its content,
which like astonishment should be
sanctification, becomes, as time declines
(with possible indications of its absence),
a usurious tax on all apartments,
into which a theater director has arrogantly moved.
Only fraud is a certainty here. And the spectator,
who has prematurely crept up like a Saint George dragon,
warms himself in the bile of the critics...
And those who dare to map even desire
have it easy, although they too are
a choleric testimony to irredeemable jackasses...
But nature is always a sign
which, if it doesn't keep silent,

denies itself. After all, the male,
that opener, feels mute only because
the spirit always moves forward
and everything closes behind it...

He too was like that... Hamlet!
His arm torn off, evening rolled through
the empty sleeve of his coat
as through a blind man's genitals, chewed up by the music...

Nature joined our contempt for the city
to the rocky urine of upturned mosses
at the entire golden height of capability
and waited until the wine caterpillar became a butterfly,
but to no avail,
because he felt contempt for wine from the day
when out of thirst he had to open a horse's artery
and drink the blood...
This led him to accept a jinni
and to exclude seemingly unrevealed mysteries,
and, being between himself and himself,
he spoke for the abyss.
After that, he only spoke out of it,
even when, say, he discussed a certain saint
who had nothing left, except her pain
from remembering an ancient lover,
a pain so small she could easily hide it
inside a rotten tooth...

It matters little
whether the saliva hissed at us
dripping from the mouth of sleeping crickets,
constructors of midnight bridges,
the created creating, who built two tombs
out of apparitions, taking a wage for prophecies.
Only art was without excuses...

And life too insisted,
but insisted with the risk that we'll survive,
although we might also wish to die...

There was no rest... Nowhere, not even in the unconscious...
But he was there, Hamlet, who like a Mozart-swigger
overturned the Alps, to place a bottle insecurely
on the creaking step of his fear of death,
so close to himself that between him
all immortality could fit...
And indeed, in his presence
the knife under the sheep
could not slash anything
and the melted pewter from old baptismal fonts
would congeal into a vital shape.
Yet anxiety exists. He was on the wound of eternity
and had to heal it. He was in his father's tomb
and had to be a son of the children... He was
with the holy sound of music
and was made to be the earnings of a harlot
or the price of a dog...

Oh, not that he knew everything, for he keenly sensed
that when selfishness stuffs itself
it does not throw up, it digests and starts up again—
not that he was wise, like a wood
pillar tends to be among those of stone—
not that he shuddered with disgust facing
an ancient floor painted by the bloodflow of women—
not that out of avarice he recalled final things
and would therefore dwell in Atreus's tomb,
in which treasury led directly into mortuary—
it mattered not to him
if Alexander the Great's crooked nose
straightened out something in history—
no, no, but I still see him scowl at people

for whom if anything is a mastery
it is also an emptiness, into which they hurl
all their emasculated fury...

Whoever gives remains avaricious...
And yet, we do not believe and are always waiting for something,
possibly people are always waiting for something
only because they do not believe... They are enlightened,
but they do not radiate... They are anemic,
as if without bloodshed there would be nothing,
they are expelled but not yet excommunicated,
they are curious but have yet to find the mirror
in which Helen-Helen
looked from below-below,
in fact, they are so deaf, they would like to hear
the voice of Jesus Christ on an LP...

And yet everything, everything here
is miraculous only once:
only once the blood of Abel
which was to wipe out all war,
only once the unrepeatable unconsciousness of childhood,
only once youth and only once song,
only once love and, simultaneously, being lost,
only once everything against heredity and habit,
only once the untying of agreed-upon knots and hence liberation,
and only once the essence of art,
only once everything against prison,
unless God himself wanted, on this earth,
to build a house...

Over the wall the greenery arched
and cast, along the way, the hawthorne of its curiosity.
The window opened the wind, which drafted through:
    All your action is a lot and is nothing,

yet action filled with being: a miracle to envy!
The night smoked history, ate the fried winglets
cut from Mercury's ankles
and washed them down
with the sweat of the organist at Saint Tragedy's...

"Only when you reconcile yourself to death," said Hamlet,
"will you understand that everything under the sun is truly new...
Our body is not a canvas hangar
out of whose fabric things can be clipped...
But our subconscious plays games... Even if we unstintingly
give alms, it is for our benefit!
Ditto for copulation by mistake... But no!
The fumbling genitals of interrelations can do nothing more in people
than to be in them without them... However,
the liver of lovemaking lies in sin.
So the penalty of the spirit will be recalled to you
even by the tension of bodily profanation...
We don't feel good around sleeping people either,
because we don't know where they will stop,
while we are stuck here...
If a man considers how heavy a cat suddenly becomes
when it is dead, while someone
can spend a whole day shooting sparrows!...
But yes, there is man shame and woman shame.
A man cannot bear to look at a cotton pad.
And a woman? Hardly born when it is dry,
she's already flattering the downpour..."

After a while Hamlet added: "For children, an answer is never enough...
For example, they play with a cupboard of secrets
and end up carrying off its key in themselves.
Or they are ailing and secretly open the letters
of an imprisoned poet who, behind bars,
paid for a special room by the fact that they themselves opened the letter...

Or they are ailing and see in dreams a pillar of fire
and cry: it's a rod, God's vein!
Or they are ailing and cannot shake from their minds
the unending handiwork of women
which may have wanted to warm only them
or to weave a man in, or to plug itself up...
Or they are healthy! It's a precious moment
when the sliced bread seems to belong to no one...
Then they'll walk out of the barn and unwittingly trample
the last kernal of last year's harvest
so that immediately they might be even more tempted
to place the gold wig of a haystack on a skull of fire.
They are as full of life as a horse
who feels the rider not as another being
but as his own thought... Rejoicing, shouting,
they've been together for a year and do not regret it,
they have a potent antidote for anything that is not a miracle—
all stains are only mud
stains on new clothes and can soon be removed...
Children! They've found the true names, which now just need
to be pronounced!"

I interrupted, saying
that he looked like a millstone quarry.
Have a drink, Hamlet, I say! Do you want it with the oven,
the mind of a farm, or
with the passion of the blood's cardinal points?
But he wasn't offended, and said "Pö-pa!"
What? say I, and he replied:
"That is what the Tibetans call themselves!"
And went on: "Virgins, oh yes,
they know when a tree is ailing!... But I have met convicts.
It is enough to imagine that some of them have
huge rumps so immense only because
the constantly rushing memory of the same crime
forces them into a legless squatting,

unless they became swollen from frequent whippings,
for they smell of tar...

'The streetcar didn't come!' says the woman. And the man
answered: 'It's worse when a ship is late,
that is, you who like a ship
leave within you under you an uninterrupted line... '
Yes... Whereas virgins, yes,
they know when a tree is ailing... And the constricting male grafts
always occur around the canvas of their innocence,
even though they already go about in harlot-hair stockings...

Freedom, you know, is always kin to
voluntary poverty..."

Night overlapped night... Inclining toward earth
or becoming a headstone for everything
that the living and the dead were doing at the time...
Maybe the living were timid and insolent...
And the dead were not intentionally, but hereditarily
or revengefully envious...
I understood when Hamlet, not suspecting my thoughts,
said: "What merely surrounds us now will one day bury us...
Once I was at a fire...
the innumerable flames made me notice
a single knuckle on the whole hand of the master of the fisheries there,
enough for me to think of the bony
carving of nothing upon nothing...
The hair of a hanged man
is even more sensitive, because fluffy on the spine,
and it is no more to being
than body hair to knowledge.
But still more spacious for the shivering quinine of Elsinore
was the sound of nails being clipped from Ophelia's feet...
You know..."

No, I don't know, I said... but right now
I'm expecting guests! I added, annoyed
by my conviction that he loved his unhappiness...
But once again he was not offended and went on:
"Querer la propria desdicha... But what
makes a mother quiver
would shatter galleons at sea...
Besides... If there is no God,
no angels, and if after death there is nothing left,
why don't those admirers of nothingness
honor precisely them, the non-existent?
I felt that once
while hunting white falcons... The feeling also rises
out of Chinese tombs... And the tablets of Moses
speak of nothing else... But from an inverted humility
or pride still unclear,
for the bellows are only now being stitched,
we'd rather kiss a greyhound between the eyes and horse on the hoof,
and when we enter a library we are not afraid...
While hunting white falcons I felt a rhythm,
before the tablets of Moses a movement,
before Chinese tombs a rhythmic harmony,
before the Ainus near, far, light and heavy gods...
Anyway, that is the moment
when you are expecting guests, and they are
already here, for they've come earlier...
Yes, to see each other and to be able to talk
and to feel intimate warmth,
and a heartbeat as true as Rembrandt's needle,
when nevertheless each of us is different
(for that is what souls do)
and not to catch the serpent with another's hand.—

A jet engine is not for a poet...
And as a tree remains a tree and still produces fruit

that ripens prematurely
fruit on time and fruit only later:
no, one cannot rush in words,
for we were not and are not
from the people's right of torture
longing to be man for man!
Efficient love, you know?... Dailiness is miraculous...

The greater the poem, the greater the poet,
and never vice-versa!" he added, then continued:
"And you are a great poet, if you ask, with whom to be damned...
Art as a work, so you don't become vain...
I tell you: art is a lament,
something for someone, nothing for all,
for simply, by hoping, you are in the future...
Something always extends beyond us, for love too
is only part of our certainty... Atonal harmony...
And pain as punishment for the fact
that pain too is fleeting...
Or is it maybe that human help
which could be a help,
uses God's help as an excuse?
I don't know, but through the *shape* of some people I realized
the proportional content of the octopus..."

The wind blustered through the chimney... And somewhere in a grove
ruffled the hair on the penis of a fallow deer..
And somewhere in history it chased the gluttonous galleons of
    Walter Raleigh,
at last to slash them apart,
just as your mother, out of impatience, once tore
her sleeves listening to Wagner's music...
But you can't force the soul out with drink, like a gopher from its hole,
because even if you think of one so well-stacked
that you whisper: quick! into the stockroom!— you're still a creature

fixed in transient shape
by the winged hate between man and woman...
Hamlet broke in: "A salamander in fire!"
Then, frying the seed of the Logos in the melted
bacon on his tongue, he hissed:
"What the poet has written, the angel or demon will do...
Thus do dreams take revenge on uninterrupted consciousness!

I'm still looking for that soup kitchen
whose food window is not the wicket in a cell door,
a wicket through which the imprisoned are observed,
that peephole called the Judas...
'Who doesn't work doesn't eat!' Yes,
but what is work? To be true to one's unselfish lot—
or to be a salesman of indulgences
or an ardent stoker in a crematorium,
to inset a thermometer into the rectum of war
or to have to sing at a vintage
as proof that you are not eating the grapes,
to inspect horses' teeth or like a hangman
rip out the nostrils of creatures before they swing,
to be corroded by vinegar and bile and take revenge on others
or burn off women's right breasts
to make them better archers,
to be the seed of fate in the womb of history
or a feeling sentenced to drudgery
under the grey Siberia of elderly heads—
or even under the threat of losing your throat, to file through your chains,
and rather gouge your eyes out
that they not see today's horrors,
and yet to hear those long dead
but free singers?...

The compositional net at best catches an ornament...

I am not indifferent to

one little step, to a single fall
of a child into the nettles... Even if his mother tells him:
go and get some rum for the tea,
off he goes, repeating to himself: rum for the tea, rum for the tea,
until he ends up whispering: tum for me!...
no, no, I'm not indifferent to a single
fall of a child... And still evil climbs
humanity's spinal cord, as covered with bloody spittle
as the stairsteps to the dentist's... It is ancient that evil
and weary, and at each step it winces but climbs on and on to
    the brain of pride,
for after so many attempts
by saints and poets,
after so many attempts by saints and poets to switch off the current—
it believes only in the harmonious moment
when there's a short-circuit
between heaven and hell.
But of course... We can also wait
for something to bang and for love to fall on us...
Or assume that hope lies in patience
and long-waiting... Imagine
life's last stop...
An old man stood there, cowering
like a word in the rain...
'I'm a waitin'ere,' he says, 'for the gentleman,
he promised me an apartment, he said it's unfurnished,
that's fine by me'—
It rained. And the old man's trust
was so blind, or so magnanimous,
that it *saw* only a rosy future
and only the bystanders understood
someone had fooled him
at the *mezzo-rilievo* of the moon... But you know how it is:
suddenly nothing, absolutely nothing,
absolute nothing approaching us,
nothing, which is like the moment when it seems

even the future is behind us.
Whoever loves should rejoice!
Yet the universe though allegedly finite
is still limitless... A man is suddenly despondent,
a woman frigid, hence they haven't killed each other,
they come together and are grateful
that once again they catch a glimpse of fate,
even though it leads
shamelessly to the poorhouse..."

And Hamlet continued:
"When an abandoned man consoles himself,
he may in the end wave with a gleaning hand.
But if he sits as a couple, he has too many
words and gestures, since before a witness
he emphasizes his suffering... And only in death
are both his words and hands forever crossed
and he is silent... But is he happy?
Happiness! Have you a note from the doctor? I *don't understand!*

Even if there were no God, even if there were no human soul,
even if there were a soul, but it was mortal,
even if there were no resurrection,
even if there were nothing left, really nothing,
my own as well as your part in such a comedy
would again only be compassion, compassion for living
which is only breath and thirst and hunger
and copulation and sickness and pain...

Once, walking through a field of blooming heather,
I overheard a child-like *why?*
and I couldn't answer.
And I still couldn't answer today after all these years
at the half-relief of the moon,
because an answer is not enough for children, nor a question for
    adults.

When my childhood trustingly accepts me,
I can't help singing.
When I think of Christ's crown of thorns,
I am struck dumb with horror.
When I look at a thorn bush and see a bird's nest,
I prick up my ears.
But when I get to know a man,
I can't help weeping...

Lament and song, and poem and music...
Imagine someone
who has been searching for his friend for a long time
and learns that he is in such and such a hospital...
What does he do? He makes up a batch of the nicest presents
and hurries to visit him...
But when he discovers that it is a mistake,
and that his friend is still missing,
he asks the first patient he meets in the corridor
if he happens to know someone
who has no visitors...
'Why, that's me,' the patient exclaims, 'that's me,
nobody's visited me for a whole fifteen years!'
The visitor makes him a present,
but the two of them in the corridor are no longer alone,
for at that moment they are enviously, hungrily
surrounded by nearly all the patients
who, with almost vengeful if not truthful obstinacy, insist
nobody has visited them for years either...

Half a kingdom and a princess's hand!
A girl recently wrote to me
inquiring if she should go out into the world
or (like invisible fruit)
wait for the last tree in the world the height of a young man...
I wrote back in the snow under her window

to wait until Mozart again
expressed the throbbing of a heart in love
with double violins in octaves...
She wrote back: I'm way beyond that and I know very well
that for Janáček timpani were enough
to express a woman's sensuous life...
I replied that for death
a clarinet melody would do... I know I was being ornery
but that girl did not care
and lives and will live and wait,
wait with curiosity, even though she knows
the bast is stripped while in sap...
You'll say to a child: Shut the door!
And he: What's coming?
—Marsyas's skin, darling!

"Women!" Hamlet said, "Eve, Lilith,
Kobolda, Empusa, Lamia!"
Whom did you name? I asked.
He said: "Why one woman of all the women
of Adam!..." And he continued:
"Women! That seemingly fleeing word, nakedly stopped,
threw its garments into the hands of our desire
and said: I am not love!
Everything then looks as if it were
bloodied cotton, kissing-place and milk-stand,
an exciting beginning to a male climax
which begs on its knees in the snowy mud of the bedsheet,
a fifth thumb into two thighs,
a warm pine cone into a cold oven,
a duel of two blind people
slamming into frontal hatred
behind backing up crab forms,
when even a murderer meets his nemesis...

There is no knowledge... We live in nothing but delusions.

And still we are aquiver with anxiety
that not even they will remain
—or that they will remain with us forever
in a smell, when the glow which put a lover in the sun
suddenly seemed to wed a beaver worker... or
a treatise on prehistoric dogs...
All this between paste-board covers... Yes, of course!
And immediately we are different. Ourselves. On our own.
And immediately we are death... Death in the jungle... He'll grow
a beard and no one will recognize him...
And she with the loveliest folds in a perfectly simple garment
will let her nails grow to release more easily
the firmly-held green slope of children's laughter...
The autopsy will then note with a reservation:
when will you forget, soul, that you have yet to be seen?
And when will you remember?
Then those who stay behind will light lamps for a whole year
while a blizzard, with its right hand
in the chimney sleeve, puts on the whole house...
And at the very moment they want to show they're not afraid:
fear has appeared out of the blue, but fear,
fear to say that and fear not to say that,
fear at the Negro music of raindrops
thumping the burdock leaves,
fear of the squirrel peeling a pineapple-like cone,
fear of the nurse who does not know the phone number
of the doctor in the very next room,
fear of the Three Kingly smelting of lead,
fear of name-days, feminine and masculine,
fear of wealth which desires something more precious,
fear of freedom and fear of the poet
who guided Eurydice out of the underworld.
For Orpheus, leading her away, *did not look back*
and so brought her back to this world.
Once here, they took several steps:

ORPHEUS: Are you glad?

EURYDICE: I don't know, I don't remember yet... I'll have to relearn pain... How long was I dead?

ORPHEUS: I wasn't really brave... Six months yesterday. It took me half a year to decide...

EURYDICE: Quiet! The world will collapse from all these heroic deeds dragging their entrails behind them!

ORPHEUS: I'd gladly tell you!... But you see: I remember everything too well... I don't know how long I've been alive... My god, you seem to have a hard time walking...

EURYDICE: It's nothing... I've lost the feel for those shoes you brought me... Those
high heels! And it's as if
my skirt were tied with I *believe in one God*...
That's a tree, isn't it?

ORPHEUS: An aspen, darling! Your favorite!...

EURYDICE: Alas, I see only its roots
(those—as you'd say—nerves of vegetation demons),
I've become so accustomed to being down there,
all I can see are its roots... But who knows!...
You said: Darling!... What does the word *apeiron* mean?

ORPHEUS: Infinity!

EURYDICE: O yes—the extension of abbreviations...

ORPHEUS: You're trembling!... You're so frail! Come and sit down here, on this stone... Take my cloak...

EURYDICE: You said: Darling!
O yes—down there I was about to forget
when suddenly I thought of your words,
in the underworld next to the stream of oblivion
is a stream of memory...

ORPHEUS: Did you find it?

EURYDICE: I didn't look for it... The deepest being
is in the unconsciousness overcome by love...
Its anguish for you,
its sympathy and bliss and truthfulness
to have you here again with me, helping me, radiating

everything that we cannot know about ourselves...
ORPHEUS: Only as a mirror... Speak to me, speak!
For that is how I know you are back on earth...
EURYDICE: True! Fuses are blowing... I see
a sunbeam lighting
the ugly scar on your left cheek,
I must kiss it... is someone following us?
ORPHEUS: Everything you left behind here...
And curiosity is here too, leaning forward like a statuette
on a car's hot-tempered radiator... Don't be afraid,
say something!... May I kiss you?
EURYDICE: Remember when I once...
Is love mortal?
ORPHEUS: I do not know... There are trains that stop
neither at local nor at main stations...
That's a rough comparison, though... Don't believe it!
EURYDICE: Down there we asked after the soul
and everything answered with a lost body...
ORPHEUS: Yes! Up here I kissed
all your nightgowns. The only scent some had was that
during your own nights you did not sleep... Others
were so sprinkled with your powder
I might have pulled them from the flowerbed... And your skirts
    and blouses!
It's insane, but I divided the space
of my memory only
by your no longer entering it... I was afraid
that my solitary recriminations
would in the end encounter their own enchantment...
Luckily, we had Juliet...
EURYDICE: I'd forgotten!... Tell me: is she alive?
ORPHEUS: Yes!... Her childlike darkness today
mimics yesterday's night... I can't
imagine what she will do when she sees you...
EURYDICE: She doesn't remember me... How old is she?
ORPHEUS: Six years east of your voice!

EURYDICE: But you said I've been dead for half a year!

ORPHEUS: Darling, you know that a man who has never been afraid
does not know what woman or volition is...

EURYDICE: Then you lied to me...

ORPHEUS: Yes... But you're alive... Imagine when she sees you...

EURYDICE: Juliet did you say?

ORPHEUS: Yes, Juliet... a little girl... something
between vision and appearance... Like you...
But when you meet (like two children
placed on the threshold of an orphanhood), you will enter
the warm interior of a house...
There are too many books in it, I know... But
it also has statues and pictures
and a sofa and a piano
and a table animal drinking the carpet's colors...
it also has your humility, which noting
much disorder, will brush off the dust
and prepare dinner...

EURYDICE: May I kiss you?

ORPHEUS: It isn't time yet, darling! For some time now
I've been observing that you were listening only
to circumambient singing, waiting for one
of those virtuoso birds to lose his voice...

EURYDICE: Fateful to yourself, how you understand me!

ORPHEUS: You are within me... Overwhelmed, I do not ask
why we are... What use is volition
in a dream that has ceased being vigilant?
I can sleep at last only because
I want to awaken somebody else tenderly... We are, darling, we are!...

EURYDICE: Juliet!... A little girl!... I know:
she was little more than a year old when I was dying...
The trees were bending the tops of the wind... Was it
astonishment, or a scream? I prayed to God:
for her, for you! I regretted
everything, I felt compassion... But
what in mercy is not pardon

would gladly interpret the foreign language of both...

We are on the verge of blasphemy...

ORPHEUS: In this way, the forest wanders in us and meets the trees.

EURYDICE: There was only a single tree and a little flower...

ORPHEUS: You know what kind... In a moment, you will smell it...

EURYDICE: She'll be starting school soon, won't she?

ORPHEUS: In a month, darling...

EURYDICE: Does she have a primer? And a blackboard and a sponge

and a slate pencil?

And a schoolbag with a little mirror inside?

Come, we must hurry... Who is

with her? An aspen?

ORPHEUS: Oh god... The aspen, wait,

why yes, Martha, you know? Old Martha... the nanny...

EURYDICE: Her? Is she still alive? Back then,

she had to have straw around her entire house,

like a house in which

a woman lies, moaning, yearning for silence.

ORPHEUS: Old Martha is with her...

EURYDICE: You speak like this now, you

who foretold the eclipse and diverted the currents of rivers?

But... I wonder if you know... if you know

that I died gravid

(as you used to put it, tenderly, in thought)?...

ORPHEUS: Come, darling!... No!... I'll carry you

and kiss you... I'll kiss you and spoil you,

carry you, carry you, carry and kiss and spoil you...

But the poet does not know how to go on—

and people have stopped fearing..."

I understand you very well! I told Hamlet... For I

once unwittingly interrupted a couple in conversation,

and they never returned to it...

They were husband and wife, both standing

in the gateway to the city of Daus...
Even though I could not immediately disappear
(so blinded was I by the force
of her beauty!), even today, after twenty years,
I torture myself with remorse...

"Yes," said Hamlet, not listening to me,
"but woman's beauty and man's longing!...
Maybe what felt terror in him during the day
found the courage to go out into the night... But later,
blind, he guides himself using a hand silvered from moth killing
or with true lunacy...
But they've already kissed him:
the hangman, the waiter with poisoned wine,
or suicide...
Whoever survives will get used to it... Or will grow wise
and bite Judas in the knee
and will not give a cent toward a burial stretcher for the poor...
you know those storm clouds sentenced to the executioner
who will shave their heads at Vulture Castle—?
They greet each other in Latin, and then it rains...
And the rain will wash it all away...
And again the sun and again man, who
on a brewery-horse hunts skylarks with a pigeon
as well as the touch of not-his-woman.
A bunch of riff-raff from nones to vespers!..."

The window opened the wind, which sang:
    Little clouds are sailing, sailing,
    inspired by cosmic space,
    but when their drops are released,
    it only rains on a snail...

"I would like to find a torrent which boils

in its waves the first cottage
built of tea-bricks—
I would like to find a river
which is, along its entire course,
without cities... Simply it is always the fear
of being alone, being alone, of simply being alone—
and so once again the woman ship and a man
who ignites his two lamps
under his lighthouse!...
And then that bewildering pause,
evoked by the entire score,
It is contemporaneity creating continuity,
a continuity that is vegetative and therefore dancing,
but so worn out that a feeling for lies
takes precedence over a thought for truth—
and then touches of little thunders
(about a child's handful)
and touches precipitously oval and hairy
like a barbershop floor before it is swept,
touches unsure of all that threatens to remain—
and then, coarseness negated by tenderness and the gentleness in
    violence—
one way or another, it is always our blood
which reddened those who condemned us—
and it is the seed that conceived: *screened*,
and it is a fruit grown embittered as a thrown fist,
and it is melancholy
replacing a step with a staircase so quickly
that it leads to the abyss,
while somewhere spurned harmony waits
like a sobbing echo with a kerchief of fog in hand,
a hand which does not know if the body's memory
will find the place forgotten by the instincts of a soul
at a loss as to whether any hint
indicates a threat: to them, *those amateurs!*

Love!... It dares, before it lives,
and always destroys what gives it life... Upside down snow...
But snow under the heel of the angel of abstraction
does not melt... And since fate is not curious about ideals,
there is ruling and there is government... But love
should be what it will be... And it is love
that tells us that we are even now condemned...
Even absurdity is absurd...
We have no choice...

The inexplicability of a sentence
which in its darkness we haven't understood
sometimes bursts into so many sparks
it blinds us... it is precisely the real
that is metaphysical... But lovers
do not like it when between a riddle
and the possibility of a solution
wit gently breaks off its own sharp points... Literal-minded,
they embrace and kiss and do not suspect
that risk too turns into habit and indifference.
For otherwise they would have to die. To die perhaps
without the master stroke of horror, but with utter certainty
in that barefoot quiet that comes toward us
in a floral invitation
and simply says: enough!
Then we only glimpse each other—
without knowing if it is a matter of alternation or metamorphosis,
we must grant both a deadline
for proffered hands and bowing,
so that meanwhile both of them can reshroud...

But a genuine lover will not make a truce with a portrait
and is unlikely to carry a cock to the Assyrians
from a word not yet begun, an uttered but unfinished indignation,
and an unstated joy... Every notion
is alluring... Even the notion of suicide...

Let the night last, then,
in which a hardened harmony
repeats its rhythms so long
that fate alone rends its female squinting
in the twinkling of an exterminator demon!
Let the night last, in which everything is in disgrace
except art, which has long been damned
by the curiosity of hells and the indifference of this world!
Let the night last, even if the stone
of the lighthouse builder were to crush his son!
Let the night last, even if during the excavation for a subway
the first mid-summer fire-fly were put out!
Let the night last, in which the whisk of a shooting star
has long since swept away the fallen she-angels
from the Vatican gardens to the forest of souls at Waterloo!
The heart is the weight... Reason only the scales... Even in
    posthumous innocence
we are tried again and again!... So, let the night last!

And it does last... Only one place is lit up:
the ballroom, that wombcave of hell and jealousy,
with the stabbing of the virginity of music
more cruel than the rape of a virgin... If an angel fought for us,
he would say just as we do: well, here you are, my little Mary,
dancing with others? How is that possible? Come!—
But she, because Eve is fighting on her side, responds:
I am not dancing, I mean... I'm afraid of words... and...
    you... you're insane!
Perhaps! he will say, beginning to draw back from her
with the cruciform horror of a painter's easel,
the horror of having to bear the image of this woman...
O yes: this very woman! And he leaps
—knowing that wine too is often cleansed with a scourge—
and slaps her face along the body
now provocatively protruding opposite her soul
and denying the promised tithe on frontal things...

Or he will force her to swallow both engagement rings!
Or he will remind her: 'like a crab, you could go backward,'
and then frighten her with a knife lacking a point
although long sharpened on a boat lacking a harbor.
Or... but we aren't likely to change the original shape
of a bicycle or a revolver...
Or a shot will ring out and he'll mutter: I've killed myself...
Or a shot will ring out and he'll mutter: I'm a murderer!
O to *see* the human voice, to *see* it just once,
at the moment it says this! The voice that until now
always lamented or accused,
the voice which caressed, lied, and trembled, humiliated,
burdensome to itself, or sated,
the voice long awaited, or thrown into
the corner of the genitals in Priam's palace
like an acetylene torch
shining on one of Helen's pubes,
the voice which suddenly feels *not even this is knowledge!*

Meanwhile, in the ballroom, blood is wiped up with a tablecloth
whose tassels quiver and maybe make a difference
between avidity and pride, disgrace and guilt,
and jail and prison for the gentleman from Incognito...
However, he just stares... It seems he's gone dull... For his shame
was in his mother's loins, then he grew up
and now male-female looks at the dead woman and whispers:
'The years go by and the linen too grows old!' And as in an empty flat
from which someone was quickly removed,
some bills remain—they will pluck him up like a bill
and lead him out...
Dett dichter nennt und keene
heile Hose am Arche hatte..."

You lived through that? I asked Hamlet...
"Only once!" he replied... "There is only one
                    love only once.

Love is truly mortal!" And he fell silent.
But because he looked like an actor not given a curtain call,
I was sorry for him and pulled him out of tragedy
into the possibility of *speaking his heart*...

"No!" he said. "There are
no more trains for Loves' Labour's Won...
and I do not feel like crossing the borders of recollection
in the top boots of poetry. But Marlowe,
Marlowe, he knew something about it... everything
occurs only once, only once!
But Marlowe, he knew something about it... and that
add a little music and we'll be moved...
Absurde! Ridicule! Dégoûtant!"

But while somewhere in the distance
lightning puked into the window of a storm,
Hamlet was persuaded, and drinking
the pitch of his idea continued:
"It was at the end of Lent... Something
for one of my crazy columns... I was struck
with a bishop's mitre from the pulpit,
and so scientifically, that I felt the gender differences on my
     skull...
I'm for exaggeration, but, of course, Hyperbolos was a notorious
     demagogue:
the most beautiful girl in Verona was ravished.
I loved her unto the eternal non-ending
and now that I hear pages turning in the scandalarum book,
I feel overwhelmed by my *chastity*... Go ahead and laugh...
Scalded in cold water,
I waited in uneven rhythms until the river froze over...
A fever-heaver hastened it...
Crazed, my shirt over my coat,
with patches on the fleshy and the bony,
I took off for Juliet's...

It happened to be market day,
but not a soul was in sight, so the doorman was content
with a bag of ginger and a card table...
He let me in... The entrance was like a stirrup held for an
    archangel
mounting the horse of architecture...
My heart was pounding like an oil painting on tin...
I entered... How gorgeous she was!
How her beauty for me was always at its beginning!
How there was no need to decide!...
How widely my longing ranged!
How the riddle did not insist on being guessed!
How the eye with no witnesses kept on trembling
so that no one could see! How astonishment went wild
and was miraculously restrained!
How belchphemously the whole world looked like a brewery while
    I drank wine!
How I absolutely disregarded what to realize
or embody!... Without impulse,
without reason, without consequences, or fate,
she was a creature of indivisible fullness...
Alas, only glimpsed: beauty is a loss
unless it repeats itself for so long
that love too becomes loss.—
At that moment, through the open window, I heard
the night steet-sweeper amassing
orange peels and hematite...
Shit above, soul below! it occurred to me.
Both are invisible...
Then, as an individual, having forgotten the mob of
    street-sweepers,
I asked her if I could play.
And I went to the piano and played
Hamletiana... Some twenty minutes
(tamquam in meridie staret sol)
I played so impetuously

I seemed to be tugging out of the notes
those cruel florist wires
which stop roses from developing...
She rebuked me... We bickered...
We bickered at first with dry hatred
but soon as if we'd stayed in dressing-gowns
throughout a sweat-drenched day...
while the cycloid of a sinusoid sentence abandoned a star
and, becoming human, started to smell...
Then I told her why I had come...
It *was you!* she cried under herself,
as if she'd had a color in the night
and let it into her voice...

Why didn't I paint her back
with a right hand full of rings?
Why didn't I dance the billy club dance,
or at least the broom dance, with her?
Maybe it would have been enough to have stabbed
her eiderdown and then split
through a lovey-dovey door... When I think
that Lope de Vega bunged his musket
with the poems he composed for Elena Osorio!...
But suddenly behind my back I felt a cloud,
if a cloud can be a demolished house...

If anything remained in the garden
my left hand felt it
like a shock of woman's hair;
if anything remained in the cellar,
my right hand, that archwaiter,
gripped the bottle... Alas, it was her throat...

Juliet!—When murderer meets murderer, they don't kill each
    other, no sir!

A girl desires and does not know, *because* she desires...
I first noticed her in the forest outside of Volterra...
It was before All Soul's Day and she was snapping off
the *least* colored twigs from the bushes.
Has she a sister or a brother? I wondered at once,
she was so beautiful that even then I was jealous...
Her body against my midnight lived so naturally
that, maddened with passion, I could not be jealous out of love.
Virginity! And I fallen among the fallen!
The great standing mirror of the air
was returning the sleep of the heart to the Etruscan gods...
Not to frighten her, I coughed.
She turned, and was calm.
Her joy was still in the guardian angel
and her happiness not yet in the demon.
As if her soul was the body of the soul.
Virgin! What God invented, he wants deeply felt!

No sonnet can be sugary,
even if written by Shakespeare.
But many are poisonous,
although not composed by Gongora...
That is why I remained silent, also because
in nature even walls have ears
and because we use death
to live even worse.
You know the rest... She was *not* my lover...
Otherwise, *my brain* today would not be finishing
its meal of forgetting... And also, *there* was no room
let alone space...
Then I remembered my *mother*
(I was her twelfth child), and though shod by fate
in leadboots, I rushed toward her
wearing dead Mozart's clothing...

Mama! She always stood on the platform of parting
and, in the end, alone! She enters
through the smallest door when we're in trouble,
one night would not be enough to celebrate her,
even if the stars with one hand raised the car
she sat in so that, rushing
to her child, she arrived before her anguish,
while the darkness went mad,
somewhere a lit window stupidly squints
with a yellow eye on the cheese of Buddhism
and ominous forebodings like the greasy cards of an omnipresent
    sorceress
seems to decide destiny by a Mariazell candle...

Mother! Her patience, her again and once more
could postpone eternity,
if it were no longer that eternity...
Her hesitant soft steps when you were ailing
or when she brought bread and was ashamed that God's gift
once again had a badly baked crust! In fact, she went through life
voluntarily and prodded by dread...
failing to wait for the light within her
to straighten up its back! And she gave everything
even if you never will read her name
in a newspaper published for beggars...
But by then the primus stove (like the crop
of a carrier pigeon) had begun to bubble
and then spurted like a sneeze in funeral silence—
and the convalescent asked with contempt if man
really does descend into the ant heap of the world
only to beg there for his own bones...
But no, *mama* was here again and suddenly said:
Christmas!—even though, in fact, she'd been saying it all year long...
And when the miracle came to pass, she was still apologizing,
saying: today of all days it didn't turn out right,
the soup is bitter with bile, the fish smells like mud,

the strudel crust is hard, don't you realize, my boy,
I can't cook anymore...
And she was there ahead of you, pouring the wine,
and then for the first time you noticed her hands,
that they'd aged, were wrinkled and veined,
those humble hands, hands of the Order of Minims,
hands so light they seemed to enfold the temptation of wings,
but hands true to everything here on earth
which like a pillow must be fluffed up
under a son's head, even if he is a murderer..."

Yes, I said, but where were your hands
when in the Tuileries you chatted with Robespierre
as to whether the gallows should be baptized
(and the gallows were!)—
where were your hands if not
where the brain is worn on top of one's hat,
where were your proud hands that prevented
a crown being placed
on the head of Poetry,
where were your proud hands that left no traces
either in a manuscript, or even
in a posthumous edition for unborn non-readers?

"Kif, shira, fasah, sibsi,
diamba, dasha, hajum, riamba, mori!"...
What were you mumbling? I asked.
"Just some names for hashish,"
said Hamlet and went on:
"I once told a woman: come on, let's go for a bounce,
I have a mattress stuffed with shorn nun hair
and I live on the 5th floor...
Someday, she said. But when she appeared in front of my building,
she didn't know how to run up the stairs.
She was a harlot from the steppes...

174

I don't know, but irony doesn't die from a love for tragedy...
Odysseus isn't tragic, Ajax is; not David, Saul;
not Faust, Mephisto... And before me,
before me there was only Alcibiades, the drunken Alcibiades,
saffron colored, anguish colored..."

Dawn began to break. Said Hamlet: "Daybreak, that whore!
But in time she seems too big to me..."
I said: That's because you're thinking about her!
He said: "Maybe!"
I said: If you like,
I'll loose the darkenings for you,
though into space,
and by means of your unguarded movement at that...
He said: "Everything, except man,
in the lightning of nature! He has found his stage,
and that does not interest me..."

But by then it was daybreak... Hamlet's right eye
bulged when dawn threw into his left eyelid
a hill on the horizon where several stones were
attempting to recover a whole castle...

"Not long ago," Hamlet said, "I was with several young people
at the aging Shakespeare's in Elsinore...
He read us his poems... We smoked them,
drank them, and praised them, we were sincere,
and declared our love for him, we longed to hear more,
and when he spoke to us about books
we celebrated him as God's own librarian—
but he never found out what we said
when we went out into the street from the casa del poeta tragico...

Of course, not even ignorance means happiness...
But a poem is a gift!"

{Prague, 1949-1956, 1962}

[My gratitude to Josef Horacek for some corrections on an earlier version]

Antonin Artaud:

Seven Works

Revolt Against Poetry

We have never been able to write without triggering an incarnation
of the soul, but it was already formed, and not by us, when we we
entered into poetry.

    The poet who writes is concerned with the Word and the Word has its
laws. It is in the poet's unconscious to believe automatically in these laws.
He believed himself to be free and he is not free.

*

There is something behind his head, around the ears of his thought.
Something is budding in his nape, where it existed even before he began.
He is the son of his works, perhaps, but his works are not of him, for what
there is of himself in his poetry was put there not by him, but by the
unconscious producer of life who chose him as its poet and whom he him-
self did not choose. And who has never been well disposed toward him.

*

I don't want to be the poet of my poet, of that alter ego that wanted to
appoint me poet, but the poet creator, in rebellion against the ego and the
self. And I remember the ancient rebellion against the forms that advanced
against me.

*

It is through the revolt against the ego and the self that I rid myself of all
the evil incarnations of the Word which were never anything more for
man than a compromise of cowardice and of illusion and who knows
what abject fornication between cowardice and illusion. And I don't want
a word that comes from who knows what astral libido that was totally
conscious of the formations of my desire in myself.

*

There is in the forms of the human Word some predatory operation, some predatory self-consumption in which the poet, focusing on the object, sees himself eaten by that object.

A crime weighs on the Word made flesh, but the crime is in having admitted it. Libido is animal thought and it was the animals who, one day, were changed into men.

*

The word produced by men is the idea of an invert buried by the animal reflexes of things and who, through the martyrdom of time and of things, has forgotten that the word was invented.

The invert is a man who eats his self and expects his self to nourish him, he seeks his mother in his self and wants to keep her for himself. The primitive crime of incest is the enemy of poetry and the killer of immaculate poetry.

*

I don't want to eat my poem, but I want to give my heart to my poem and what is my heart to my poem. My heart is what isn't me. To give one's self to one's poem is also to risk being raped by it. And if I am Virgin for my poem, it should remain virgin for me.

*

I am that forgotten poet, who one day saw himself fall into matter, and the matter will not devour me, not me.

I don't want those aging reflexes, the product of an ancient incest due to an animal ignorance of the Virgin law of life. Ego and self are those catastrophic states of being in which Living Man allows himself to be imprisoned by the forms of himself that he perceives. To love the ego is to love a corpse, and the law of the Virgin is infinity. The unconscious producer of ourselves is that of an ancient copulator who indulges in the basest of magics and who has discovered a magic in the infamy of endlessly reducing oneself to oneself in order to make a word emerge from a cadaver. The libido is the definition of that cadaverous desire and fallen man is an inverted criminal.

*

I am that primitive made unhappy by the inexpiable horror of things. I don't want to reproduce myself in things, but I want things to be produced by me. I don't want an idea of the ego in my poem and I don't want to recognize myself in it.

*

My heart is that eternal Rose that grew from the magic power of the initial Cross. The one who crucified himself in Himself and for Himself never came back to himself. Never, for this himself through which he sacrificed Himself he also offered to Life after having himself forced it to become the being of his own life.

*

I want forever only to be that poet who sacrificed himself in the Kabbala of the self to the immaculate conception of things.

—Rodez, 1944

[My gratitude to Deborah Treisman for crucial corrections in a draft of this translation.]

Pounding and Gism

The words we use have been handed down to me and I use them,
     but not to make myself understood, not to finish emptying
     them out of me,
then why?
Just because I *do not use them,*
in fact I do nothing other than keep quiet
and pound.
Other than that if I speak it's because of fucking, I mean
     the universal fornication continues which makes me forget
     not to think.
The fact is that I say nothing and do nothing, that I use
     neither words nor letters,
I use no words and I don't even use letters.

I have never founded, started or followed a movement.
I have been a surrealist, that's a fact,
but I believe I must have been so in deed,
and indeed I was one but I wasn't one when I initiated or
     signed manifestos
unless it was to insult

          a pope,
          a dalai lama,
          a buddha,
          a doctor,
          an academic,
          a priest,
          a cop,
          a poet,
          a writer,
          a man,
          a pedagogue,
          a revolutionary,
          an anarchist,
          a cenobite,

a hermit,

a dean,

a yogi,

an occultist.

As for the reactionaries, the fascists, the communists now in
power, the rightists and the leftists, they won't even be insulted,
they won't even be broken up, won't be decomposed,
those bastards, the way we say: nature does it, it's her
process, but that's not enough, and there is something more
serious to be done in that case.

So then, so why once again a tract from you, Artaud, and why
haven't you gotten the hell out since you've been given the
sign to get out.
"Make way for the young, for the newcomers, for those who
have nothing more to say but who are there.
The situation stinks."
It's precisely that it doesn't stink enough to keep criticism,
or attack, or judgment, or aggression of any kind away from
me.
And why the hell should I care? In fact it might mean nothing
to me at all and I might contemptuously disregard it but
the trouble is precisely that it does mean something to me.
I mean that the nuttiness springing up all around me does not
leave my body unscathed, I am infected with it as if by
variocccele, by blennorrhea, AND I DON'T LIKE THAT ONE BIT.
Style horrifies me and I notice that when I write I'm always
producing it, so then I burn all my manuscripts and there
remain only those that call to mind a suffocation, a gasping,
a strangulation in I know not what lower depths because that's
true.
Ideas horrify me, I don't believe in them any longer
and I want them to be stirred up
and for people to say I am crazy: crazies bite, right?
So let the disputator come,

he'll say to me: this exists, that doesn't,

and things are like this or not like that,

I bite him,

for I really do not believe in words or in the ideas stirred up
  by words, and inside of words,

to be means no more to me or LESS than not to be, and nothing
  no longer means anything to me,

and silence as well, no more and even less.

And it isn't that I'm neither to the right nor to the left for
  I'm even less center and I hate equilibrium even more than
  deportation,

on condition that it's I who carry myself away, and I get carried
  away when I see the unchanging center approaching.

For I see clearly that certain people are beginning to hold it
  against me that I'm old hat.

I hate philosophy, magic, occultism, esoterism and yoga, as well
  an anatomy,

ANATOMY I say, and medicine, arithmetic, algebra, trigonometry,
  differential calculus, and the precession of the equinoxes,

and as well, though no doubt no one will believe me, a gut hatred
  of poetry.

I've received lots of anonymous letters in my life. The last one,
  sent just a few weeks ago, told me of the mailing of an old
  poem that I never received, but it only gave me the title
  without comment:

THE LAMENT OF OLD ARTAUD ASSASSINATED IN THE OTHER LIFE AND
WHO WILL NOT COME BACK AGAIN IN THIS ONE.

For fear no doubt that I might forget that I was back and welcome back.

Another letter chides me for writing in French, in good French
  I mean, and for using flowery language like the rest. Nobody
  has reproached me for being dialectical or dogmatic—as for
  dialectical I don't know what it is. But finally I too have

been approached for also believing in verbal superiority,
for attaching a value to sentences that are solidly constructed,
elegantly strung together, full of rhythm and well grounded.
"And that, I've been told, makes us laugh, the way
you believe in beautiful French."
"You attack authority, society, religiosity, and rituals as if
those words still hid facts and idea. And above all you believe
in words, in the strong words you use. Nothing but the
void has ever meant anything, you are full of yourself and
full of everything. Beat it."
I must say that I am the one who translates all these criticisms
into studied French, for the young people who have addressed
me in this fashion have done so only from a distance, as if
from one edge of space to the other, or by mail, and have
only made obscene gestures at me to prove to me that I was
on the wrong track, for close up it would have come to blows.
But they haven't yet dared to risk that.

So I must say that over the thirty years I've been writing I
haven't entirely found yet,
neither my word nor my language yet,
but the instrument that I've been ceaselessly forging.

Feeling as I do like an uneducated illiterate, this instrument
will not be supported by letters or alphabetic signs, there
one is still too close to figurative, ocular and auditory
convention.

Whoever has tied up meaning, tied up thought, and whoever has
tied up meaning thought, has tied them up in terms of a preventive
ideation whose formal written tables—tables of perceptual
significations—were inscribed upon the walls of an inverse brain.
For the human brain is no more than a double which by projection
emits a sound for a sign, a sense for a sound, a sentiment
for a sign of life, and idea for a movement, everything
is written, lived on astral matter and letters are only movements

that require a little bit more of the great film to unreel its unveilings.
A printed letter is an obsolete movement which once again comes
    to project the gism of a terminal phosphorus,
and soon all letters will be read,
all letters completely exhausted.

And each book written will be read, and won't be able to say
    anything anymore to those totally decomposed brains, after
    being arbitrarily imposed and re-imposed.

ALL OF THAT IS VERY WELL BUT I HAVE NEVER FALLEN FOR SUCH
    NONSENSE.

For letters are no more than the simplistic graphism that might
    correspond to the necessity of being awakened by the reflex
    spectre of an organ created for a certain time and condemned
    at birth:
                    THE BRAIN.

The lobes of the brain are not infinite, neither is the infinite,
    but it lasts.

I know a state beyond mind, beyond consciousness, beyond being,
                    in which there are no more words nor letters,
but into which one enters by screams and by blows.

And it is not sounds or meaning that come out,
nor words
but BODIES.

Pounding and gism,

in the infernal blazing mass where it's no longer a question of
    words nor of ideas.

Pounding to death and fucking the face, gism on the face, is the
last language, the last music I know,

and I swear to you that bodies emerge from this
and that these are *animate* BODIES.

> ya menin
> frat e sha
> vazile
> a te sha menin
> tor menin
> e menin menila
> ar menila
> e inema imen

{September 1946}

189

Civil Status

It's me, Artaud, Antonin
fifty,
       who does it,
taking the skin, and splitting it,
instead of waiting for its physiological rehabilitation by
     some watchfiend-like new daddy,

just as when vertigo occurs,
I don't attribute to god
       the straightening out of the father's children,
but first of all
I let the merinos piss, while kicking beings about, so they'll
     get away from my fire,

for I am, as everyone knows,
that great genius
      the one who says so,
      who wrote,
      not the Kabala,
      the Popol-Vuh,
      the Brahma-Putra,
      the Kama-Yoni,
      and Ji ni ini ini
      of all the imputed yogis,

but this avant mamtram of filth,
      of pestilence
      and of pus
through which life
      suppurated
advancing toward the wall of hardened spasm
      and of sleet
that the ever-benumbed head cold

        of being
grates to death
when it ripens
the tongue of its inflammation

                                    {November 1946}

Letter to André Breton

Around the 28th of February, 1947

Dear friend,

You bitterly reproached me for my performance at the Vieux-Colombier which was the first occasion that I had found to tell the public of this society what I thought of them,

which had kept me interned for 9 years,

my spinal column demolished by its police with blows from iron bars,

had me struck with a knife twice in the back by pimps,

arrested and sent to prison, deported,

had me attacked on a ship,

kept incommunicado for 3 years during my first 3 years of internment,

had me systematically poisoned during 5 months in one of its insane asylums (that of Sotteville-les Rouen, October 1937– March 1938).

Perhaps I did gather people in a theater, to do so,

but to say that I remain a man of the theatre, as you say I do in your letter, by the mere fact that I appeared on stage,

is a gratuitous injustice

for I do not believe, no matter what boasting there might be in saying it, that any man of the theatre since the theatre has existed had adapted before me the attitude that I had that night on the stage of the Vieux-Colombier, and which consisted of belling on stage hateful eructations, colics and cramps to the extent of a syncope etc.

Outside of gathering people in a hall,

it also remained for me to castigate this society in the street,

but it's difficult since the streets are filled only with hurrying passers-by, and to invite them to listen one needs barricades and bombs,

but how is it that you did not *notice* that on the Vieux-Colombier stage I myself realized the inanity of my attempt and giving up the idea of reading the lecture I had prepared I packed my bags and left,

hurling into the public the last stanza of a poem:

> all the yoga exercises
> are not worth the desquamations
> from the cunt of a dead tench
> when the wench who flaunts it
> pisses while quartering her tit
> in order to cross syphilis

for I suddenly realized that the hour had passed to gather people in a theatre even to tell them truths and that with society and its public there is no longer a language other than that of bombs, machine guns, barricades and all that follows.

But how after that, André Breton, and after having reproached me for appearing in a theatre, can you invite me to participate in an exhibition, in an art gallery, hyper-chic, ultra-flourishing, loud, capitalistic (even if it had its funds in a communist bank) and where all manifestation can only have now the stylized, limited, close, fixed character of a tentative art.

In a gallery one sells Painting, one buys paintings, it's a trading-post like the Jesuit trading-posts in India or that of Lally-Tollendal,

the objects on display are put in a box (in a coffin) or in show windows, in incubators, that's no longer life;

all the snobbism meets there like, alas! at the Orangerie they met before van Gogh who deserved a much different evening.

For there is nothing that topples cosmography, hydrography, demography, the science of eclipses, of the equinoxes and the seasons as does a painting by van Gogh.

No, I can absolutely not participate in an exhibition, and especially in a gallery,

all the more so because there is one last thing in your project that lifted me from my seat in horror.

This parallelism of surrealist activity with occultism and magic.—I no longer believe in any notion, science or knowledge and especially not in a hidden science.

Regarding nature and things I have my personal idea, and it bears no resemblance at all to anyone else's whoever he may be and I do not allow civilizations, nations, religions and cultures to come and bore the shit out of me with their conceptions, and to tell me: Well, here's the last word on the profound nature of chaos and cacophony, on injustice and the crime of the created, what has been found by your fathers the buffoons and what is, think under the carcan of the 12 housed Zodiac.

(For why not 13 or 19 and why houses and not garbage dumps of shit, swooning abysses.)

I have my own idea of birth, of life, of death, of reality, and of destiny, and I do not allow any others imposed on me or even suggested to me,

for I do not participate in any of the general ideas on which I could have with any other man than myself the opportunity to meet myself.

You have therefore separated this exhibition into 15 rooms, with an altar in each one, modeled, you say, on those of Voodoo or Indian cults,

and representing the 15 degrees or stages of an integral initiation.

It is here that my entire physiology rebels for I do not see that there is anything in the world to which one can be *initiated*.

All experience is resolutely personal,

and another's experience can serve no one at all outside of himself without the risk of creating the sordid alter ego dusthaze of which all living societies are composed and where all men are brothers in fact because they are cowardly enough, unproud enough to want themselves extricated from something other than the same and identical cunt,

from a similar cuntish slut,

from the same irreplaceable desperate and stupid cuntishness,

which is easily seen through since everyone is from birth forced to think the same thing about the greatest number of points.

A fine way moreover to lose authentic reality, the universal, to restrict oneself to the knowledge of a particularism of castrates and pedants which has been done by a very limited number of individuals.

Notwithstanding that I believe there is no universal reality, no absolute to be known, and to which one must be led, that is to say, initiated.

Initiations have only suceeded in enclosing us in those ignoble ersatz

yo ana
ka nemkon
nestrura
kom nestrura
kahuna

of explanation of a cosmic mechanism that does not exist, and of the revelation of a so-called Pulcinella secret jealously buried under the defecations of a few pompous braggarts who have lived only by their lies and the naiveté of those dodos who followed them.

There is no cosmos and each man is his world to himself alone,

it's up to him then to initiate himself in making it live, that is to say by creating it, with the arm, the hand, the foot and the breath of his personal and inexpugnable will.

Who does not want to initiate himself to himself there is no other who will initiate him.

And there is only one sun, one moon and stars only because everyone yielded on this point about universal light to the conceptions of that phenomenal hood named god, instead of doing as in the real world where each individual enlightens himself on himself, as did van Gogh in order to paint the night with his 12 candled hat. Everyone preferred to laze around without working to be enlightened by the profit of the rape of this consortium of pedants,

the demiurge and his assessors.

The human body has enough suns, planets, rivers, volcanos, seas, tides without still going to seek those of so-called exterior nature and others.

Surrealist activity was revolutionary on condition that all be reinvented without any longer obeying any point of any notion brought by science, religion, medicine, cosmography, etc.

And there remains on this point a revolution to be made on condition that man does not think himself revolutionary merely on a social level, but that he believe that he must still and particularly be revolutionary on a physical, physiological, anatomic, functional, circulatory, respiratory, dynamic, atomic and electrical level. And in order to achieve that cease to believe himself mortal and destined to the coffin after 100 years of life which is the average figure chosen by priests from the year 1000 and imposed by them on all humanity. For before the year 1000 everyone did not die and there were in that epoch villages and towns called living dead where men heavy with several thousand years still lived, rejected by the church for the simple fact of being alive.

For me that is the only revolution that can interest me but, it is a U T O P I A, is it not, which fails to realize that such a revolution cannot, especially this one, assert itself without bombs and machetes, without iron and without blood.

None will initiate me into anything,

first of all because it has to do with me and about myself I know more than anyone else,

second because outside of myself there is nothing except other men with or without egos,

but no nature, no cosmos, no principles, no essences, no general truths, no universal foundations to a being of things, which does not exist.

No man has on the plan of life

in order to meet another the intermediary of an idea, notion or common perception.

It is arbitrarily that one created sensations, sentiments, emotions and pass-key notions that when one pronounces words like love, honor, liberty, truth, everyone believes they understand each other and think the same thing while in fact there is nothing that separates one man from another more than notions

of love, honor, liberty or truth.

That is why I do not believe that there is an occult world or something hidden in the world, I do not believe that under apparent reality there are buried and repressed levels of notions, perceptions, realities, or truths.

I believe that everything and above all the essential was always in the open and surface and that this has sunk vertically and to the bottom because men did not know and did not want to maintain it.

That's all.

The occult is born out of laziness, but did not become occult, that is to say irrevealable, because of that.

Add to that, André Breton, that by the fact, and because of all that I think about these points, for 10 whole years I have been in open struggle every night and day with all the sects of all the sorcerers and initiates of the earth, 10 years, exactly since I made the journey to Mexico to the Tarahumara Indians where I had to battle for 28 days at an altitude of 6000 meters in order to suceed in personally approaching the preparers and manipulators of Peyote.

No, there is no occultism and no magic, no obscure science, no hidden secret, no unrevealed truth, but there is the bewildering psychological dissimulation of all the tartuffes of bourgeois infamy, of all those who ultimately had Villon, Edgar Poe, Baudelaire, and above all Gérard de Nerval, van Gogh, Nietzsche, Lautréamont,

and who could have had Coleridge too if the latter hadn't committed the arrant cowardliness of turning himself over to them, tied hand and foot.

And who also had Lenin whose unclear death was due to a spell undoubtedly proceeded by poisoning.

There is no occultism, no occult magic, but there are *spells*, obscene ritual spellbinding maneuvers periodically set up against certain consciousnesses in which all of society participates not just with its unconsciousness in complete abandon, but indeed and in all consciousness, and then makes use of certain other maneuvers, first obscene, then mathematical, to hide it, and to hide it from itself by forgetting it.

Life, really, is not absolutely what it appears to be, a series of sunny days, then days of rain, of mist, of clouds, of snow or wind, there are also "atmospheric" variations of another order that take place, not everyday of course, but from time to time, at certain hours of the day or night, and which are the hours when the maneuvers I speak of take place, where consciousness raised all over the earth is visible across the spaces as from street sidewalks to each other, and where all the accomplices of a same social filthiness recognize each other and pass each other the word.

This makes for 2 to 3 minutes of trouble, sometimes a quarter of an hour, sometimes under certain solemn circumstances an hour, a half day or night, but this does take place; when it involves uniting to strangle or suffocate a strong will, a great heart, all the sexes of humanity recognize each other from afar and know how to thicken, to knot themselves, to contract, to stretch, to distend themselves to produce certain scleroses, certain voids, certain stupors capable of suffocating or maddening a genius or a great heart.

How many times does one not wake in the night as though between two dreams and doesn't one have the sensation of being plunged into a real world, authentic, but different from the ordinary and everyday world,

and in the morning when definitely awake one never fully knows if it was a dream or reality.

It was a reality but an extra-ordinary reality in the midst of which the consciousness of the masses sports at ease and does the harm it has premeditated.

It is above all in these hardly ordinary states of nocturnal repose that all the great outcries of consciousness of which I speak take place, where one decides the strangling, the alienation, the paralysis, the internment or the suicide, of Gérard de Nerval, of Nietzsche, of Lenin, of Villon, of Lautréamont or Edgar Poe.

How many times in the past 10 years have I myself not found myself caught up in similar tides, in any case often enough, and bitterly enough to have remained completely conscious of them and to never never forget it.

Whereas those who abandon themselves to it forget it.

"Such a person," says Rimbaud, " thinks he is a man,

he is a dog."

Me, I say:

"So-and-so thinks he is an honest bourgeois, he is in reality a hypocritical spellcaster and has done what was necessary to no longer even know it, a fine way to no longer have to defend it or have his secret taken from him."

So I became conscious of all of this and I absolutely swore to myself that they would not do to me what they did to Gérard de Nerval, to Lautréamont or to Lenin,

and I learned how to make use of certain methods of attack or aggression which precede all the possible mass conscious risings against me,

for which the masses do not forgive me.

Knowing how consciousnesses get close to each other across the spaces I also learned how to take them by surprise, to look at them closely, to hear them and to see them.

Thus for the past 10 years I have on me and I see around me an insane horde of corpuscles, animalcules, fluidic bodies, moreorless spectral figures who have no other worry, no other purpose than to act against me as ghouls, lemurs, vampires, and to ceaselessly exhaust my humors, my secretions, and my vital juices.

Thus I have purulent testicular eczemas on eczemas, rhinituses on rhinituses,

aqueous hemorrhoids on hemorrhoids,

this could renew all the stories of incubuses and succubuses of the Middle Ages if I didn't know that these incubuses and succubuses are priests, doctors, scholars, administrative employees, small shop keepers and also the upper bourgeoisie, monks, rabbis, lamas, bonzes, brahmans, yogis etc. etc.,

that is to say everyday men.

Therefore as an enemy of all human magic I can absolutely not participate in a manifestation which so-to-speak sacramentally and without clowning evokes its rites, its settings, its "triangulations" and its carcan.

> **na ina**
> **ta tia nantifta**
> **tia nantifta**
> **tia ita**
>
>
> **ta rupta**
> **ta rupete**
> **e tifta**
> **e te tifta**
> **eta bita**

I do not want from a fake cosmos's anatomy someone to extract a skeleton the glove of which I will force myself to put on.

While I know that I myself have made for myself a body a lot more inhabitable and livable than this carcass of demented buffoons:

Voodoo or Ciguri sorcerers etc. etc.

The current human body is a gehenna that all magics, all religions and all rites have implacably set upon to sclerosize, to tie up, to petrify, to garrot in the module of its present stratifications which are the first real obstacle to all real revolution.

It is very probable that after this you will once again turn your back on me as happened between us in 1925, that you will spit on my carcass and my ideas, will vomit me from head to toe, however I can have no other reaction.

I think of the horrifying parade of uncultivated snobs that will circulate through this exhibition, and will find only a small way to mentally masturbate more. For I have the sinister impression that the huge bourgeois masses now believe themselves mithridatized against the idea of pure surrealist danger. And that this no longer prevents them now from burying both ears in their pillows.

That is why it was not without a *deep rolling malaise* that I heard you tell me the other evening in the café de Flore that you were *hostile* in advance to the idea of my performance at the Vieux-Colombier.

If there had only been the fear that you had of seeing me arrested again, it would have been nothing and I would not have been disturbed,

but, to tell the truth and as one who knows how to detect atmospheres, that fear that day, at that moment, was no longer in *the air*, one sensed perfectly that there would be no question about it.

There was on the other hand something else in the air, it was *fear*, confirmed and admitted fear, of seeing me, me, make certain precise accusations, against certain persons tied to the order and to the game of Institutions and their representatives, of seeing me make certain revelations concerning the game of the occult police of those sacrosanct Institutions, and concerning certain monstrous practices to which the organic lower depths of everyone's civic unconsciousness habitually abandon themselves.

To be hostile to the idea of this performance was to be hostile to it in this sense and for this sense, otherwise why hostility, why the word *hostile?*

To fear for my health, my life, my liberty, does not arouse a hostile feeling, and that particular word is beside the point, hostility is enmity, and unless you are my enemy for the reasons I mention above one couldn't think of showing oneself *hostile* to the idea of the performance at the Vieux-Colombier.

Moreover it was to terribly misestimate me in not believing me to be capable,

me,

of resisting a public or a crowd;

you will tell me that this public and this crowd already got me once

since they imprisoned me, deported me, put me in a strait-jacket, interned and poisoned me, and kept me interned for 9 years.

Possible,

but there are circumstances which have to do with simple human honor, no matter the risk,

to resist and to not cop out.

I was arrested and imprisoned in Ireland

because I wanted with that simple cane you know about to resist a huge crowd and the entire Dublin police force.

Society got me that day but after 3 days of battle and they never openly spoke about those I wounded, mutilated or killed.

Afterwards if I have been interned it was because *once imprisoned, I simulated* madness for an hour in front of a state security agent, after having received a visit from an emissary of a group of initiates, who asked me to sacrifice myself, and to undergo a period of confinement, privation and maceration,

in order to correct my body of certain vices, of certain aberrations, of certain sins to which *in my very body* a large part of humanity believed itself to be attached.

And I haven't mentioned again to you that I had undergone at that particular moment nauseating spellbinding influences which had incited me to convert, and that I had done it.

Since then I've renounced my baptism

and only those who had me baptized could be hostile to the idea of certain revelations,

but not you,

after all,

no,

not you

André Breton.

I gave this performance only to reveal the tumors of present society from the angle at which I know them.

I can't stop myself from doing this

because I want to live

while men of the present earth

prevent me, *me, from breathing.*

I chose a theatre because I didn't have at hand another public place,

and because before passing on

to the final attack

I also wanted to gather my friends and to know who I could count on.

Very well, there must have been about 10 people in the theatre, the rest are good for nailing on pitchforks.

I wanted a certain number of people to become conscious of something with me.

Very well, once again the strident hypocritical and occult dishonesty of the universal spirit had acted up, something tied itself onto me, rushed into the air, against which I would have needed not words but a machine gun.

The hour, André Breton, is very near when one will have to fight, really fight, physically, bodily, but this time

unto death,

I mean without fear of death.

If somebody had said to me: André Breton is going to address the crowd, he's risking his skin,

I would not have said: I am hostile to the idea of seeing him go to the crowd,

I would have said: let him go, I will come and attack the crowd with him and be mutilated or massacred with him.

At this hour I no longer believe that it is the question of my own massacre, but of that of a crowd of sperm drinkers, of exsanguine, exhausted masturbators, of integrally emasculated and emptied psychurges.

For this world issued from a crime no longer knows anything about the methods employed to lead it to a good end. And which were not eternally valid anyway, although it believed them to be.

World sprung from a false hundred nails, which believed that it could draw eternal ideas from certain chance explosions.

For I do not want to finish this letter without telling you that the gravest protest that I have raised on earth is that which I raise against *eternity.*

And which never was, on the part of the spirit without body, and thus without the merits of work, the revindication of a duration and of a reality which could never have been, because they can around and in relation to the same and identical fact be calculated, by 10 hours as by 10 minutes without the value of the fact being objectively changed. Which is the most crass and most monstrous injustice, in the absolute.

When a worker has worked 10 hours he has done more work than someone who has worked 10 minutes, and at equal value it is he who has worked 10 hours who has done the best work and has done the most work.

Well, it seems that in the eternal this is not true.

Very well, dear friend, I think that my insupportable dissertation will cease to appear trifling to you if I tell you that eternity is the means that the insipid spirit of god has taken to preserve itself confronted by the sapid and laborious human body, and you will answer that you don't give a fuck,

neither do I,

but eternity submerges me and asphyxiates me and you too.

It is because eternity still exists in spite of Rimbaud that you've never been able to live and that *André Breton has not had the life that he should have had.*

Ignoble fraud of the ritual phlegm of the priest spirit, contemplative gear work of the human individual, ignoble vengeance of the impotence and the cowardice of those who could not enter into man, truly be men and who wanted to justify, and to consecrate their life of spirits. Ignoble and criminal violence, odious rape of those myriad clots of corpuscles
cultivated
by certain races of men, on the model of certain races of monkeys and animals,
faculty of emitting in the air bodies which resemble their own bodies, in certain states of erotic febrile over-stimulation, or in psycho-physical, physico-dynamic, magnetic-psychic trances, the Chaldeans, then to forget the departed bodies and conceal oneself in the work of everyday life, men believing that in doing this they are imitating me, me, as though I had bodies that turn around me all day long, coming out of me from all sides in order to be and to claim an existence,
while the bodies that they saw around me did not come out of me but from the earth where I had sweated and made caca.

To lean on the force of time until such a point of pain that it can no longer hold within itself but disengages outside
and holds itself suspended outside of all notion,
but it dies,
thus my misery must have come to me from what I imposed on myself one day
too great a pain
that my body
was not able to tolerate
and
and it jumped,
which all the beings in hell took advantage of
and jumped me
and I wasn't able to completely dominate them
and I had to again find a body that was proof against absolute and infinite pain,
it is now done.

It remains for me to finish checking the revolts.

For once I jumped

the beings who started,

the beings who started one day,

those who would have liked to be good and to love me were not old
enough nor numerous enough to resist the others,

that is to say the hell of unnamed beasts

(and the unnamed beasts, so goes the legend, have invaded all of
humanity)

well, no, that's false,

men have eaten of the beast and filled themselves with beasts

(to live eternally).

narch indalizi
dalsk aldi

They *educated* themselves in nothing, they are automatisms against nature
that certain men suffered in the false body and repeated afterwards.

My true state is inert, far beyond human life and captation, it is that of
my body when *He* is alone.

.

Note

Artaud's famous performance at the Vieux-Colombier took place on the 13th of
January, 1947. The next day he wrote this letter to André Breton who had expressed
certain fears relative to this performance [This letter was published in a magazine
called le *Soleil noir*—Positions, n°1, February, 1952]. The surrealist group was then
preparing the 1947 *International Surrealist Exhibition, presented by André Breton and Marcel*

Duchamp, which was supposed to take place from July to September of that year. Breton wrote Artaud and personally invited him to participate in this exhibition, the purpose of which was "to reaffirm a true cohesion and relative to previous group exhibitions to mark an advance." The spirit in which the exhibition was conceived involved translating "a new myth" and the framework had to obey "the primordial question of retracing the successive stages of an initiation." The ground floor rooms were to be occupied by "a retrospective entitled *Surrealists in spite of themselves.*" The upstairs rooms were to be reached by "a 21 step staircase modeled after book spines, whose titles corresponded in meaning to the 21 major divisions of the Tarot (with the exception of The Fool)." The staircase led to "the Hall of Superstitions" which was followed by another room divided into "12 octagonal cells," in the order of the signs of the Zodiac, each of these cells being "consecrated to a being, an order of beings or an object thought to be *endowed with a mythic life*" to which it was suggested "an 'altar' be raised, modeled after pagan cults (Indian or Voodoo for example)." It is to this invitation that the letter of Artaud relates. Both this letter and the information for this note were translated from *L'Ephémère, n°* 8, Paris, 1969. The letter here is followed by four more which have not to my knowledge been translated. An early version of my translation of this letter appeared as *Sparrow* 23, Los Angeles, August, 1974. This final version, with the help of Bernard Bador, was completed in 1993.

Ten years that the language is gone,
that there has entered in its place
this atmospheric thunder,
      this lightning,
facing the aristocratic pressuration of beings,
of all the noble beings
      of the butt,
cunt, of the prick,
of the lingouette,
of the plalouette
           plaloulette
           pactoulette,
of the tegumentary trance,
of the pellicle,
racial nobles of the corporeal erotic,
against me, simple virgin of the body,
ten years that I once again blew up the Middle Ages,
with its priests, its judges, its lookout,
      its priests above all,
      its churches,
      its cathedrals,
      its vicars,
      its white wafers.
How?
With an anti-logical
      anti-philosophical,
      anti-intellectual,
      anti-*dialectical*
      blow of the tongue
with my black pencil pressed down
      and that's it.

Which means that I the madman and the momo,
kept 9 years in a lunatic asylum for exorcistical and magical passes and

because I supposedly imagined that I'd found a magic and that it was crazy,
one must believe it was true,
since not a single day during my 3 year internment at Rodez, Aveyron, did
the Dr. Fredière fail at 10:30 AM, the visiting hour, to come and tell me:
Mr. Artaud, as much as you may wish, Society cannot accept, and I am here
the representative of Society.
If I was mad in my magical passes, what did it matter to Society which could
not feel attacked or injured and had only to despise and neglect me.
But the Dr. Fredière presenting himself as a defender of that Society and
entrusted to defend it must have recognized my so-called magical so
called passes since he was opposing me with Society,
I therefore say that the dismissed language is a lightning bolt that I was
bringing forth now in the human act of breathing, which my pencil
strokes on paper sanction.
And since a certain day in October 1939 I have not written anymore without
drawing anymore either.
But what I draw
are no longer subjects from Art transposed from imagination to paper, they
are not affective figures,
they are gestures, a verb, a grammar, an arithmetic, a whole Kabala, and one
that shits to the other, one that shits on the other,
no drawing done on paper is a drawing, the reintegration of a strayed sensibility,
it is a machine which has breath,
it was first a machine which at the same time has breath.
It is a search for a lost world
and one that no human tongue integrates
and the image of which on paper is no more than a tracing,
a sort of diminished

copy.
For the real work is in the clouds
Words, no,
arid patches of breath which gives its full
but there where only the Last Judgement will be able to decide between
values,
the evidences,
as far as the text is concerned,

in the moulted blood of what tide
will I be able to make heard
the corrosive structure,
there where the drawing
point by point
is only the restitution of a drilling,
of the advance of a drill in the underworld of the sempiternal latent body.
But what a logomachy, no?
Couldn't you light up your lantern a bit more, Mr. Artaud.
My lantern?
I say
that look ten years with my breath
I've been breathing hard forms,

     compact,

     opaque,

     unbridled,

     without archings

in the limbo of my body not made
and which finds itself hence made
and that I find every time the 10,000 beings to criticize me,
to obturate the attempt of the edge of a pierced infinite.

Such are in any case the drawings with which I constellate all my notebooks.

In any case
the whore,
oh the whore,
it's not from this side of the world,
it's not in this gesture of the world,
it's not in a gesture of this very world
that I say
that I want and can indicate what I think,
and they will see it,
they will feel it,
they will take notice of it
through my clumsy drawings,

but so wily,
and so adroit,
which say SHIT to this very world.

What are they?
What do they mean?

The innate totem of man.

Grigris to come back to man.

All breaths in the hollow, sunken
        pesti-fering
        arcature
of my true teeth.

Not one which is not a breath thrown with all the strength
of my lungs
with all the sieve
of my respiration,

not one which does not respond to a real physiological activity,
which is not,
not its figurative translation
but something like an efficacious sieve,
on the *materialized* paper.

I am, it seems, a *writer*.
But am I writing?
I make sentences.
Without subject, verb, attribute or complement.
I have learned words,
they taught me things.
In my turn I teach them a manner of new behavior.
May the pommel of your tuve patten
entrumene you a red ani bivilt,

at the lumestin of the utrin cadastre.

This means that maybe the woman's uterus turns red, when Van Gogh the mad protester of man dabbles with finding their march for the heavenly bodies of a too superb destiny.

And it means that it is time for a writer to close shop, and to leave the written letter for the letter.

April 1947

I Spit on the Innate Christ

There is in the idea of christ
    myth on one side
    history on the other

The myth now
    is worth what
    some great poetic
    stories were worth,

not that it has worth
    it is false
for it does not pertain
to the story
of this true christ
who lived in Judea
about two thousand years ago
whose translated Hebrew words
    mean donkey fart,

      inchristic gas of a donkey
        anus,
      of a donkey grotto
      open further down
        in
          an-us.

In fact it is on this idea of psychism,
    of an innate
      spiritualism
          ferociously
        encrusted with things
that the whole old story
of christ has always been constituted.

It is very definitely
this story that
Jesus christ of Nazareth
was teaching
but if it represents
a spirit
it does not represent
a man
for the bottom of all
magical
psychurgy
resides in its
absolute
irreducibility
to any possible
material incarnation

the spirit is this
tall door of a body
that advances
and covers itself
with one hundred-fold lightning
to signify
that it is closed
forever.

But what then is the story
that christ was teaching

If it is on the other hand
that of a god incarnate,
of this sort of innate breath
which manifests itself
in the middle of certain
magical epiphanies

and whom a virgin
would have brought forth
in order to incarnate and
materialize him

hoek   **tibi**
   shakh   **bi**

yaz   **bif**
   che   **tif**

but all of this is neither
beautiful
          nor true
and it's infantile
       as well
like all that has been
nothing but human

If christ is god
he has no need of
a virgin's
uterus
to make the sign
that he was.

He was there but nobody
had ever looked

The story of the spirited high
door of things
is much more marvelous
and magical
to consider.

Things did not come
from a spirit-god
but from a man-man

who made them with the
hand
and with the breath of his will

but without having like christ or the
Virgin
to dig up
the badly dampened soil
of his sex
like a monkey which would unearth his newborn
with the nails of his own feet

What man wants
is
but there was never
for the holy spirit
to volatilize

———

And there is another nasty story to which
the story of the word Jesus-christ refers,
it refers to this spirit
emerged from a sex,
by the churning
of a principle
forced.

Compelled by the hand

and the tongue of man
    which suddenly passes
    a mephitic gas
    counter-irritated and
horribly diverted.

In any case what remains
of this whole christian
story
is that Jesus-christ
thus
of the family of christs
or jackass farts
to which Joseph Nalpas
  belonged
has maybe finally
founded a cult
the cult of god
who rises suddenly
or descends

but he has not
founded it with his
blood. —For
when he felt
the Jerusalem atmosphere
  too dangerous for him
  he did not stay to await the soldiers
  who could have come
    to fetch him,

but he hurried to get the hell out.

And it's another character
a kind of nobody,
much more disgusted by priests

than he who died
on the cross,
not moreover by
chance,
but for the
defense of his
ideas.

Who was this guy
a nobody I said
whose name no one knew
and whose existence
has been carefully hidden
forever by all the
priests of every age because
like them
he did not belong
to the vile and anusaire
world   The spirits,
who shelter
in their own anus
terrors
ceaselessly hatched by
the auricular
presence of
death.

This man was an unbelieving
humorist,
who kept saying that death
did not exist,
nor spirits
nor god
and that there was only man
a man
who had created all

things
        not like spirits
    which materialize or
        become incarnate
    but like bodies
    which reveal all at once
        their bodily state,
    its reassuring objective
    presence
        with no innermost depth in which
    bad conscience could
    nest behind things.

    Things were such
it is as such that they had been created
        in fact,
and if bad conscience existed
it was the priests who had created it
in order to terrify savagely
        and to hold prisoner
    any free will
    of man that could have
        desired to show itself.

        Shonauch aumal
            ato not me
                romé
                sabu
        shianbi aises
            aho ato   iniitie
                itia
            shianbi aises abiaisle
                ato   inititia

It is for that that this
    man was crucified.

His name has not been kept but he is
to be found seemingly among priests
by the noise that would make
     the breath of absolute
     invisibility,
by the state of total nothingness
  without memory nor possible return
  to a being whatever it may be

———

     non aumong amay
        may
    arhmong amay tamau

For things are always at the same
point they have not changed, it's still
the priests who hold in their
dirty hands the abyss of immortality,
as they willfully and systematically
keep this very world under
the angle of misery, the bankruptcy of
consciousness, of despair
from complete corporal starvation
and of death.

These are the priests that one day I will
really roast at the top of a wall and
embalmed roast under the nose of the people who
followed them
     ma filelta zama kabafa
    ma   kabafa
      auma   kaumon

To be Christ is not to be Jesus Christ

The story of the Eucharistic queer descended
from god's adulterated sperm made my heart
sweat enough,
        my spirit shit,
so I want to mention it,
for the part that concerns me
        and which I would say is
        the main one,
        the rest being
        only kitchen gossip
    vulgarities of the neighborhood
        and of chores
          in the barracks

        or
        rather

        NO

    and keep your paws off

      FIDO

the repugnant queer
    of everybody's
        innate beast
    and of the pussy
    of all beings

      is not going
      to continue

           to hoodoo us
          under the vile
       and pederastic *name*
                  of

       Jesus-christ

spreading out two thousand years ago from all the low
sewers of Jerusalem
and distributed universally ever since
          in derision
of any possible high spirituality,
          of all science
          and all accomplished men.

For Jesus-christ is the obscene name of the
impious doll, *the animated vampire,*
   that the syphilized lips
   of the *expert*
          matrix
     of things,
shape automatically
every thousand years, and which they're ready to
shape once again
I don't know where but I do believe it is
on the side of the Turkestan steppes
   this time,
if one does not decide to let them do it,
and if once and for all one does not lay
hands on the collars of all their dirty sorcerers
to skewer them on a
          spit
          and,
     after having fastidiously compiled them
          to stick it to them

and to bury them alive in a
broiler kept blazing.

———

We know the name of this queer of a black
magician who all christians for some 2000
years adore under the name of
     Jesus-christ,
he was authentically called Nalpas,
and belonged to a know family of
pariahs,

meaning untouchables
who nobody approached,

and not on account of their diseases,

but because of their customs which
made them sick people
of a particular kind,
    burdened with plague,
       with bed sores,
  with buboes, with ulcers,
    with tumors,
but above all with sweating and breathing
  a kind

of snotty humour,
  where snot
    mixes
with tart and putrid
    saliva
      and blood with urine,
with the liquors of internal organs

and finally with
excrement

Here is the filthy yeast of humanity,
    which never had any other goal
other than to bestialize its human state
    (and
        out of vanity believed to be
                psychurgy, did it
systematically and as if by goal),
    here is the specimen ejected from the broken-in lips
of the black matrix
for he who was called
        and is called now the
Messiah or
            christ
        (without knowing that
            christ
        meant   in Hebrew
                DONKEY FART)
and the christs were a family
of indurated men,
left on earth since the Flood
    and they remained there
    in a kind of latent state of
petrification
    between manhood and animality, which turned
each member of the
CHRIST family
into a kind of model donkey,
of born burro,
of man who has not decided for
man's life
        but could not maintain a donkey's life
entirely, and constituted this family
of pariahs that christ nurses

and where he might better have gone to
be nursed himself.

Here is I say this kind of holed puppet, this
hideous snarling iron of a man that the
christians adore under the name of
    jesus   christ   the   crucified

———

They've never been very disgusted.

———

if there is no other christ,
no other disembodied puppet who
far from the turpitudes and filths of the body,
would have descended into hell
to break the chains of a humanity
   purely moral
      and which would descend
      for 2000 years
      everyday
      onto the altars.

———

If there is a left-over it is a foetal left-over from
the lost body of things which emerge in this way
universally every thousand years
through the lips of the materialized matrix
of things,
   and how could it be if not for the
maneuvers of the dirtiest magic of

beasts

reincarnated and reincorporated

koïmonk
redi
talik
onok
koïmonk eretiki

enoch
tapo
kalen
elen
meinarok eretiki

ya   mon   lerbo
derfel
te dan
e nelezo

Notes

These two poems by Antonin Artaud were published for the first time, in 2001, by Abstème & Bobance éditeur in Paris. The poems were written in August and September, 1947, and both are pre-occupied with what Artaud called "The true story of Jesus-Christ."

Relevant to both poems is the following graffito:

Dating from the 3rd century A.D., this graffito was rediscovered in 1856 on Mount Palatine in Rome. In constitutes the first representation known to this day of Christ on the cross. The translation, "Alexamène adores God," evokes the calumny of onolatry, which attributed to Christians the adoration of a donkey. Tertullian condemned the opinion of an onocephalic man-god, *Somniastis caput asinum esse Deum nostrum*, and reported besides a rumor according to which "throughout the city, one no longer speaks of an onocoital God."

For commentary on the "syllable words" to be found at points in these poems, see pp. 334-335 in *Watchfiends & Rack Screams* (Exact Change, Boston, 1995), works from Artaud's final period, translated by Clayton Eshleman and Bernard Bador, which contains a biographical introduction to Artaud's extraordinary and terrible life.

Appendix:
Revisiting Neruda's *Residencias*

Pablo Neruda's first two *Residencias en la tierra* (published in 1931 and 1935) were my initial crucial discovery in poetry, and the first poetry that I attempted to translate. For reasons that I will explain here, by the time my translations appeared in book form (*Residence on Earth*, Amber House Press, San Francisco, 1962), I had set Neruda materials aside, and started to read and attempt to translate the dense, complex posthumously-published poetry of César Vallejo. In the early 1990s, Jerry Rothenberg and Pierre Joris asked me if they could include a couple of my *Residencias* in the first volume of *Poems for the Millennium* (University of California Press, Berkeley, 1995). I went back to my book and decided that I did not want to have anything in it reprinted, so I redid the poems they asked for. Two years ago, while composing the manuscript for this revised edition of *Conductors of the Pit*, I was again faced with deciding whether or not to include these early translations. Why not include them to show how I started off as a translator? But the fact was that they were definitely inadequate relative to my current translation standards, and some did not interest me as poems anymore. I decided to retranslate eleven more of these versions, so that I could open this book with work that I was proud of. While doing so, I revisited some of the aspects of my "Neruda experience."

In 1959, while we were graduate students at Indiana University, Bill Paden, a painter friend, gave me a copy of the 1947 New Directions *Latin American Poetry*. I was immediately attracted to Neruda and Vallejo. Since the anthology was bilingual, I began checking word choices in their selections, using an English-Spanish dictionary. At the same time, I found a copy of Angel Flores' bilingual translation of the first two *Residencias*, and compared his with those of H.R. Hays (also an early Vallejo translator) and Dudley Fitts in the New Directions volume. I had the experience that I suppose many translators have at the beginning of their careers: one of shock, at the astonishing discrepancies and outright errors (which even I could spot!) in these different versions. To some extent I became a translator reactively, disgruntled with what others had done, and with some unbased confidence that I could do a better job! My problem was that I did not know Spanish, nor anything about constructing a translation.

My first attempt to do something about these problems, and inspired by Neruda, was to hitchhike to Mexico City, the summer of 1959. Via the Beats, hitchhiking on long journeys of self-discovery (or ruin!) was very much in the air. Ginsberg had spent time in the state of Chiapas (southern Mexico) in 1954, and wrote one of his first impressive poems there: "Siesta in Xbalba" (the Mayan word for the underworld). By 1959, there were Beat types in Mexico City, writing poetry and giving readings in a couple of cafes. While attending a poetry reading, I met Al Perez and Walter Compton, two American students who spoke Spanish. Together we translated several of the *Residencias*.

Our cotranslations appeared in the first issue of *Folio* that I edited, winter 1960. *Folio* was the English Department literary magazine, with very limited distribution, and completely dependent for material on non-solicited submissions. When the editor quit, I offered to take his place and got the job, whereupon I wrote letters to many of the American poets I had been discovering via Mary Ellen Solt and Jack and Ruth Hirschman and asked them for material for *Folio*. I assembled my first issue that included Ginsberg, William Carlos Williams, Gregory Corso, Robert Bly, and Louis Zukofsky. Before it could go to the printer it had to pass muster with the *Folio* "faculty advisor," a Joyce scholar named Robert G. Kelly. Kelly informed me that the Ginsberg could not be printed because it contained the words "shit" and "fart," and that a section of Zukofsky's work, "Bottom: On Shakespeare," would also have to be pulled because it was obscure. Not knowing what to do, I called up Ginsberg and told him what had happened. He told me not to quit, that what I was doing was valuable, and that he would send me another poem to replace the censored one. Zukofsky also agreed, and offered a shorter section from "Bottom" (no less obscure than the first one, but it got by Kelly, I guess, because it did not take up much space!). The issue got published, but the word was out: the barbarians were inside the Bloomington gates. At a faculty meeting, Kelly arranged for the money to be pulled from the *Folio* budget the following year, thus ending the magazine after my third issue in the summer of 1960.

That summer I got a ride in the back of a flat-bed truck to Etzitlan, Mexico, ending up in Chapala for a couple of months. I rented a room in the home of an ex-American retired butcher named Jimmy George, who had a 16 year old Indian wife, and lots of pigs and turkeys. I showed some Neruda poems to her one day, and with her very modest English and my baby Spanish (and the faithful bilingual dictionary), we made some crude versions together, which were the real start of my *Residencias* collection. At one point I made a down-payment on a leather-bound *Obra poética completa* in nearby Guadalajara, to then come down with hepatitus. I had to beg for my down payment back in order to buy a third-class bus ticket to Tijuana, where I was rescued by James and Ann McGarrell who were living in Los Angeles at the time.

Two summers in Mexico had opened up the world for me, and now I was eager to go to Spain. In an attempt to get there, I signed up for the Western Division of the University of Maryland's Overseas Division, which supplied American instructors for college courses on military bases around the world. Maryland called me in June, 1961, and informed me that while there was no post in Europe, there was one job in the Far Eastern Division—Japan, Taiwan, and Korea. My first wife and I left for Tokyo two months later.

While living there, we hosted Gary Snyder and Joanne Kyger who were passing through Tokyo on their way to join Ginsberg and Peter Orlovsky in India for six months. They told us we could make a living teaching English as a foreign language in Kyoto, where they lived, so in the summer of 1962 I left Maryland and we moved into several rooms in an old Japanese house in the Kyoto foothills. Once settled in, I turned to my Neruda translations, a few of which had been published. I had also exchanged some letters with Neruda himself. I began to investigate book publication by sending the manuscript to Paul Blackburn in NYC, who had a year before become a kind of friend and mentor. Blackburn's big translation project, continuing for years, was a large gathering of troubadour poets, whose intricately-rhymed 12th century ballads he was converting to idiomatic American poetry. Paul liked my Neruda versions and encouraged me to publish them as a book. In retrospect, I imagine that he did not check them against the Spanish originals, even though he was fluent in Spanish. Had he done so, I think he would have found some accuracy problems.

I was also cultivating a friendship with another poet deeply involved in translation (and editing). Cid Corman lived in a rented room, and had turned a table at The Muse coffee shop in downtown Kyoto into his evening "office." I would drop by for a few hours about once a week. Cid would share letters, books, and gossip, and by paying attention, I was learning something about the life of a "man of letters," the ingredients that make up that "combined object" of writing, translating, and editing (Corman was editing *origin*, Second Series, at the time). On the basis of reading Cid's Celan, Ponge, Char and Basho translations, I was impressed, so I showed him the Neruda manuscipt too. He was not impressed: his main objection, relative to my versions, was that they were wordy, with lots of repetitive phrases, too many articles and conjunctions. What I didn't think to do was to point out that the material he objected to was in—or I thought it was in—the original too. So was he criticizing my versions or Neruda himself? Swayed by Corman's air of authority, I began to "weed" lines in my versions. For example, in 1960, I had translated the following two stanzas of "Walking Around" in the following way:

> It shoves me into certain corners, into certain damp houses,
> into hospitals where bones jump for the window,
> into certain shoeshops that smell of vinegar
> and into streets terrifying as chasms.
>
> There are sulphur-colored birds and horrible intestines
> hanging from doorways of houses that I hate,
> there are false teeth forgotten in a coffeepot,
> mirrors that should have wept for shame and terror,
> there are umbrellas everywhere, and poison, and bellybuttons.[1]

After cutting out some fifteen or sixteen words from these two stanzas, and paring the translations in general, I showed the new manuscript to Paul Blackburn again, and he wrote me that I had ruined the translation. I ended up compromising, putting some of the deleted words back in. My problem was that I lacked a translational viewpoint, so I could be bounced back and forth between Cid and Paul. It turned out that they had serious aesthetic differences which would come to light a year later. After compromising, these stanzas looked like this:

> shoves me into certain corners, certain damp houses
> in hospitals where bones jump for the window,
> shoeshops smelling of vinegar

streets terrifying as gashes.

There're sulphur-colored birds and horrible intestines
hanging from doorways of houses I hate,
false-teeth forgotten in a coffee-pot,
mirrors
that should have wept for shame and dread
everywhere umbrellas poison navels

In this version some phrases are so clipped (and unpunctuated) that their syntactical relationship to other phrases is unclear. I had tried to make Neruda's conversational lines more concentrated by eliminating words here and there. But to truncate is not to compress.

Corman's criticism of my translations reflected his own kind of Minimalism, a procedure at the heart of his poetics. Working under a haiku alter ego, he hoed a small patch, over and over, from the 1950s on, having eliminated length (I do not know of a Corman poem that is over three pages long), fantasy (and thus what I would call imagination, in exchange for keeping the poem perceptual: observation and statement), collage, politics, mythology (in any participatory sense), and Eros. His coined term "livingdying" is the controlling radar.

While Blackburn and Corman may be said to overlap when it comes to an exacting observational grid, in most other ways they are poets of different ilks. In contrast to Corman's essence, Blackburn is processual: the poem as a stretch of thinking open to those areas mentioned above that are absent in Corman's work. His poetry is full of distress and anxiety, sexual revelation, and is sometimes rather aimless, picking its way toward a nonexistent resolution.

I first began to think through these differences when origin #8 was published in January, 1963. On the inside front cover (giving it considerable prominence), Corman had printed part of a letter from Ted Enslin, recently returned to rural Maine after spending some months in NYC. Immensely pleased to be back in woodsy isolation, Enslin wrote: "I look at the city now, perhaps not as I will in time, but certain things begin to come through. Much of it, the life there on all levels, is a reciprocal disease of parasites. The sickness is highly contagious, and it results in feeding back and forth among the invalids of the sickness itself—reinfection again and again. Probably why they all have to stick together no matter how bad things get, rather than any sign of strength. P, for example, when I told him I was leaving, told me I had no defenses. I countered with, no, and I had no intention of developing any..."

"P" is Paul Blackburn, and by leaving a telltale initial in the text, Corman was clearly using such a letter to pointedly teach him a lesson (and condone Enslin's blanket condemnation of NYC citizens!). This letter is followed by a large selection of Corman's own poems. On the first page there are two short poems, one in which a child is dancing in a garden, and a second in which the speaker (presumably Corman himself) is warming his hands in rural winter (while Kyoto is a very large city, it generally appears in Corman's poetry as a kind of medieval village). Such poems support Enslin's black and white attitude toward city and country. On page two, there is a poem that can be read as addressed, critically, to Blackburn's aesthetics (with the Enslin remarks setting such up):

The Offerings

Too many things on the altar.

A petal would do.

Or the ant that stops for a moment
at it.

I recall reading this issue at home in Kyoto and thinking why does Cid have it in for Paul? And: Paul is really going to hit the ceiling when he reads this! [2]

I continued to visit Corman at The Muse weekly, and one night showed him a version I had done of a poem by the Spanish poet, José Hierro. Cid glanced back and forth between it and the original, and suggested we retranslate it together. He admired Hierro's poetry, and in tandem we worked through several pages of it. Rather than proposing cutting out redundancies (or what he had taken to be redundancies, in the Neruda Residencias), he meticulously respected Hierro's lines, word for word, and directed a translation that was very accurate, taking no liberties or short cuts. So this is what translation is about, I thought, no showing off ("belly-buttons" for *ombligos*), no exaggeration ("chasms" or "gashes" for *grietas*, more accurately "fissures"), no cutting or adding, and no explanations instead of precise translations. And no guesswork—if you don't know the word, find out what it means (even if you have to make a special trip to the library to do so). I attempted to employ this procedure in my Vallejo translating, and while I did so for the most part, it took me a decade to actually practice it ceaselessly.[3]

So, nearly forty years later, I have come back to these Neruda translations and have attempted to bring them up to snuff. I realize how powerful these image-driven poems were for me as a novice with a literal-minded background. My initial response was not that much different from Miguel Hernández's upon reading the second *Residencia* in 1935:

> I need to communicate the enthusiasm that has transformed me since I have read *Residence on Earth*. I want to throw handfuls of sand in my eyes, to catch my fingers in doors, to climb to the peak of the most difficult and high pine. It would be the best way to express the stormy admiration that a poet of such size awakens in me. It is a danger for me to write about this book and it seems to me that I can say almost nothing of the enormity that I feel. Fearfully, I write.[4]

The American poetry that I was exposed to in Sam Yellen's 20th Century Poetry class (in 1958) might be indicated by a couple stanzas of a then-famous poem, "The Equilibrists," by John Crowe Ransom:

> Full of her long white arms and silky skin
> He had a thousand times remembered sin.
> Alone in the press of people traveled he,
> Minding her jacinth, and myrh, and ivory.
>
> Mouth he remembered: the quaint orifice
> From which came heat that flamed upon the kiss,
> Till cold words came down spiral from the head,
> Grey doves from the officious tower illsped.

Given this daily bread in Yellen's class, the reader can appreciate my excitement upon reading the opening of Neruda's "Single Gentleman":

The young homosexuals and the horny girls,
the gaunt widows suffering from delirious insomnia,
the young wives pregnant thirty hours,
the raucous cats crisscrossing my garden in the dark—
like a necklace of throbbing sexual oysters
they encircle my solitary house
like enemies set up against my soul,
like conspirators in pajamas
exchanging countersigns of long thick kisses.

I about jumped out of my chair when I read that fifth line. In an instant it conveyed the force of figurative language. These poems were written by Neruda, when on a series of consular and diplomatic assignments for the Chilean government, in Ceylon, Burma, Singapore, Rangoon, and Buenos Aires. These places do not appear at all. The poet appears to be in a western city, at the same time packed with modern stuff and deserted, a kind of spectral site, in which he is profoundly grounded and alone. On one hand, he seems to have an erotic arsenal of imaginal materials at hand, and on the other, he is devastated by just how much he cannot account for. The circulating emptiness is weighted by a relentless, impure sensuality. Everything is ordinary—and fantastic. It is as if Henry Miller had gone not to Paris but to Rangoon and eaten conger eel for a year. I actually recall a comment by David Wade, a student writer friend at Indiana University to whom I read my initial Neruda translations. At some later time, I asked David what he did for poetic inspiration. He said, well, I read some Neruda, eat a bowl of mushroom soup, and then go to bed.

The reader should keep in mind that in the Bloomington of the late 1950s, for us students at least, mushrooms were an exotic, unfamiliar substance.

The most ambitious—if not the most successful—of the Residencias that I have retranslated is the "Ode to Lorca," which another Neruda translator, Donald D. Walsh, tells us was written in 1935, the year before Lorca was murdered.[5] The poem which proposes itself as an ode from the first stanza on is filled with violence and death. Lorca is portrayed as "sobbing sobbing," a state of mind clearly beyond dramatic gesture. He is portrayed, as a matter of fact, as a figure of utter despair. In the poem's fulgurating sixth stanza, a veritable army of images and friends arrive at Lorca's house.

While the title might lead to reader to feel they arrive in homage, by the end of the list the thought is likely to occur that Lorca has died, and that the grand procession has arrived to mourn a dead poet. After the arrivers are named, the poem begins to back off from itself, and the remaining seven stanzas lack impressive imagery and hobble, more and more weakly, to the final curious and foreboding statement. Why will Lorca come to learn other things—slowly?

This is an instance in which Harold Bloom's thesis concerning artistic competitive anxiety might be usefully applied. Does "Ode to Lorca" express a subliminal desire on Neruda's part for the extinction of his prime rival in the Spanish-language poetry of the 30's? Here we have an ode that is loaded with killer kisses, death in red lakes, ashen rivers, rotted crowns and funeral ointments, vinework covering bones, Lorca's own mouth of submerged blood, death among spiders, and acrid daggers driven into the bodies of those who have given up on life.

Some of my revisions are more ambitious than others. In some poems it was mainly a matter of creating a readable format and touching up things here and there. In other cases, such as "Only Death," "Nuptial Material," "Autumn Returns," and "There Is No Forgetting," early versions have been thoroughly reworked.

I moved to NYC in 1966. That fall, Neruda was invited to NYC to read at the 92nd Street YMCA. Paul Blackburn found out the names of the translators whom Galen Williams had invited to read with Neruda, and discovering that I was not one of them, convinced her to invite me. So at one point I was on stage with Neruda, reading a few of my *Residencias*. At the end of our portion of the reading (to the biggest audience, someone said, since Robert Frost), we spontaneously embraced each other. Over the next week, I visited Neruda in his hotel near Washington Square Park and Fifth Avenue, went out to dinner with him and other poets, and participated in an additional reading that he offered to do "for the poets" in the apartment of Betty Kray. I found Neruda completely accessible, jovial, and attentive. At the end of this week, some people from the cultural wing of the Chilean government who had accompanied Neruda to NYC asked me if I would come down to Santiago for two years and, for a salary, do nothing but translate Neruda. It was clear that they had their sights set on a Nobel Prize. I said no. I had left the haunting terrain of the *Residencias* for the impregnable strong room of the *Poemas humanos* which was testing me even more than poetry itself had when, as a lost soul in the midwestern 1950's, I discovered its power to change and enable one to stand more self-revealed.

Notes

1. Taken from *Hip Pocket Poems* #1, ed. by Emile Snyder and Jack Hirschman, Hanover NH, n.d. (1960, I recall)

2. While researching the Paul Blackburn Collection at the Archive for New Poetry (The Mandeville Department of Special Collections, USCD) in 1985, I discovered an unpublished poem, "To a Friend," written to Cid Corman in the spring of 1963. It opens:

Dear Cid.

No.

Too many things on the altar?

No. There are

never too many things

on the altar. Sure, a

petal would do, your offering always

was a petal, and

does, say. But you

don't understand, there are

those who must bring more to the altar..

The poem continues for another forty-two lines, and with those above establishes Blackburn's aesthetic differences from Corman's. From Blackburn's viewpoint, Corman's commitment to the art is a limited one, tips without their bases. See Edith Jarolim's note on p.121 of *The Parallel Voyages* (SUN/gemini Press, Tucson, 1986), which includes the full text of "To a Friend," along with forty-seven previously unpublished poems.

3. I offer an example of this dilemma, as it concerned the 1968 Grove Press edition of *Poemas humanos*/*Human Poems*, in "The Translator's Ego" (*Antiphonal Swing: Selected Prose 1962/1987*, McPherson and Company, Kingston, NY, 1989).

4. *The Selected Poems of Miguel Hernandez*, The University of Chicago Press, 2001, p.105.

5. Pablo Neruda, *Residence on Earth*, tr. Donald D. Walsh, New Directions, NYC, 1973, p. 171.

Notes on Certain Contributors and Cotranslators

{Only those authors and translators not discussed elsewhere in this book, or whose work is not widely-known to poetry readers, are cited here}

A. JAMES ARNOLD [Cotranslation of Artaud's *Pounding and Gism* and *Civil Status*]: Arnold is a Professor in the French Department at the University of Virginia. He has authored books on Valéry, Sartre, and Césaire. At the University Press of Virginia, he created CARAF books and the New World Studies series.

ENIKO BOLLABAS [Cotranslation of Géza Szöcs]: Bollabás has taught at the József Attila University in Szeged, Hungary, and has traveled extensively in the United States, doing research on Americana and John Muir. She has published *Tradition and Innovation in American Free Verse: Whitman to Duncan* (Budapest, 1986) and *Charles Olson* in the Twayne United States Authors Series (1992).

SANDOR CSOORI was born in Zámoly, Transdanubia, in 1930. As a poet he is one of the most articulate representatives in Hungary of the so-called "Folk Surrealism," a modernist esthetics which builds on archaic elements in folk art, and regards as its forerunners artists like Béla Bartók and García Lorca. The central theme of Csoóri's writing is the relationship between history, national and individual consciousness, and the distortions politics bring about in this relationship.

FRANTISEK GALAN (1947-1991) [Cotranslation of Vladimir Holan]: Galan was born in Czechoslovakia, and was Director of the Comparative Literature Program at Vanderbilt University at the time of his death. His books include *Historic Structures: The Prague School Project, 1928-1946* (University of Texas Press, 1984), and *Poetics of Cinema: Classic Readings in the History of Film Theory*, ed. (in preparation).

JORGE GUZMAN [Cotranslation of the first two César Vallejo prose poems]: Guzmán is a Chilean essayist and novelist, with a PhD from the University of Iowa. He is a professor in the Centro de Estudios Humanísticos de la Facultad de Ciencias Físicas y Matemáticas de la Universidad de Chile, and the author, among other books, of *Contra el secreto professional, lectura mestiza de César Vallejo*. .

MICHAEL HEIM [Cotranslation of Vladimir Holan]: Heim has been a professor of Slavic Language and Literature at UCLA since 1986. His many translations from the Russian, Czech, French, Hungarian, Croation and Serbian, include: Danilo Ki's *Encyclopedia of the Dead*, 1991; Jan Neruda's *Prague Tales*, 1993; and Milan Kundera's *The Unbearable Lightness of Being*, 1999.

JOSE HIERRO (1922-2002): Hierro was born in Madrid, and imprisoned by the Franco government in the mid-forties for "assistance and adherence to the rebellion." He was admitted to the Spanish Royal Academy of Literature in 1999. His collections of poetry include *Tierra sin nosotros* (1947), *Estatuas yacentes* (1958), and *Cuaderno da Neuva York* (1998).

FERENC JUHASZ, born in 1928, was raised in Bla, a village near Budapest. His reputation as a major 20th century poet rests on *Struggle with a White Lamb* (1964) which contains "The Boy Changed into a Stag Cries Out at the Gates of Morning," cited by critics as one of the great poems of our time. His writing is driven by a fascination and horror over the forms and processes of life on both microcosmic and macrocosmic levels, the cells and the stars, which he describes with unparalleled mastery.

GYULA KODOLANYI [Cotranslation of Csoóri, Juhász and Radnóti; author of the note on Juhász]: born in 1942, raised and educated in Budapest, Kodolanyi, much influenced by Charles Olson, writes a prose poetry that is multi-layered and densely esoteric. He is also a major translator of American poetry (Pound, Williams, Duncan, Creeley, and Levertov among others), and the editor of an anthology of American poetry from Roethke to Creeley.

MIKLOS RADNOTI (1909-1944): as a Hungarian Jew, Radnóti was enrolled in forced labor battalions after Hungary's entry into WW II. After having been moved from Serbian mines, exhausted and diseased, Radnóti was shot by guards and buried in a mass grave near the city of Györ, in Western Hungary. After the war, the grave was opened, and a notebook containing some of his greatest poems was found in his trenchcoat pocket. All of the Radnóti poems in *Conductors of the Pit* are from this notebook.

ANNETTE SMITH [Cotranslation of the last two Aimé Césaire poems]: Smith is an Emeritus Professor of Literature at the California Institute of Techonology. Besides publishing books and articles on various aspects of colonialism and racism, she has co-authored with Clayton Eshleman four translations of Aimé Césaire, one of which, *Aimé Césaire: The Collected Poetry* (1983), received the Witter Bynner Award from the Poetry Society of America.